METROS IN

railways of

MADRID

BARCELONA

VALENCIA

BILBAO

Robert Schwandl

Capital Transport

ISBN 185414 242 9

Published by
Capital Transport Publishing
38 Long Elmes, Harrow Weald, Middlesex

Printed by CS Graphics, Singapore

Designed by Tim Demuth

This book is dedicated to Felix L. Thoma.

CONTENTS

Left L–10 Gregorio Marañón – a brand new 2000-series train (small profile) on service along Madrid's new north-south line. The light grey strip next to the train is the provisional board added to the platforms as long as small profile rolling stock is used.

Right L–5 Eugenia de Montijo is the newest station on Madrid's current metro network (opened 27/10/99). It was built at the site where the original *Suburbano* line enters the tunnel between Aluche and Carabanchel, therefore daylight comes into the station from all sides. An old 1000-series train was still in service in April 2000.

AUTHOR'S NOTE

Spain is going through a kind of rail revival. For many decades mainline railways had deteriorated and the service provided was slow and unreliable. In the mid-1980s, Spain's national railway company, *Renfe*, began to invest strongly in suburban services by acquiring new trains and improving the whole infrastructure. Although still far from perfect, this was a radical change which was also reflected significantly in ridership statistics and the company's reputation. The company also began improving long distance services, but it was Spain's first international gauge high speed link, opened in 1992 between Madrid and Seville, which revolutionised Spain's railway map. Since then other lines have been improved to reduce travel times, and a 750km long high speed link from Madrid to Barcelona and further on to France is under construction.

Spain's historic metros, in Madrid and Barcelona, have been growing steadily since their inauguration in 1919 and 1924 respectively, but only in the mid-1990s did a new attitude prevail which considered a much more user-friendly metro and a real alternative to road traffic. In only ten years, Madrid will have built 100km of high capacity mass transit lines, something unimaginable in most cities of the world (except Seoul) nowadays. Pushed by the everlasting rivalry between Spain's major two cities, Barcelona is now about to follow Madrid's example and plans to construct some 50km within the next ten years. Meanwhile two other cities, Valencia and Bilbao, broke the traditional Spanish concept of metros and converted former suburban lines into modern metros by extending them underground into their city centres. Both cities are also reintroducing tramways, an example most likely to be followed soon by other cities like Barcelona, Málaga, Alicante, La Coruña and Seville. The latter is a sad example of a frustrated metro for which construction started in 1976, but due to some accidents and a fear of damage to historic sites in the city centre construction was stopped and tunnels already excavated were filled with sand. Currently the construction of a modern light rail network is planned. However, at the time of writing no definitive details are available although most known proposals include the tunnel section built in eastern Seville.

All pictures, unless indicated otherwise, were taken by the author during the last five years. As only a limited number can be published in this book many more are included on a CD-Rom which is available directly from the author. On this CD-Rom you can listen to all station names, see the networks grow and find out many more details. For the last five years I have also been the author of an extensive website, metroPlanet, dedicated to all metros around the world, where you will also be able to find the latest news on Spanish metros and more about the CD-Rom. You are also welcome to comment on anything in this book via email.

Throughout the book station names are shown in CAPITALS to distinguish them from identical place names which do not always refer to the station. This makes stations more easily identifiable on rail maps. Railway company names are shown in *ITALIC CAPITALS*. The term *metro* is used to refer to rapid transit rail lines whether in tunnels or running in the open.

A book like this has many contributors, some of which I would like to thank personally: Emiliano Durán of Metro de Madrid for guiding me around the network and explaining all kinds of details, Manuel Melis at Madrid's Office for Infrastructure and Transportation for providing a lot of material on the previous metro expansion programme, Edorta González in Bilbao for his continuous updates and for checking the Bilbao chapter, Enrique Collantes in Madrid for keeping me informed, and many other often anonymous helpers from around Spain and from around the world who have sent me emails with interesting news. Last but not least, my sincere thanks to Peter Nichols and my friend Richard Tinkler for checking the English language.

I would like to thank the following for their annual reports, maps and other material sent: Ferrocarrils de la Generalitat Valenciana, Metro Bilbao, IMEBISA, TMB (Transports Metropolitans de Barcelona), Consorcio de Transportes de Madrid.

Barcelona, December 2000

Robert Schwandl
robert@metropla.net
www.metropla.net

MADRID METRO

INTRODUCTION

Madrid has been the capital of Spain since 1561 and lies in the geographical centre of the country, 600km south-west of Barcelona, 400km south of Bilbao, 540km north of Seville, 350km west of Valencia and 600km south-east of La Coruña. Compared to Barcelona or Valencia, which are of Roman origin, Madrid is quite a new city. Although Celt-Iberians, Romans and Visigoths had also settled in the area, it was the Arabs who, in 886, established a fortified camp where today's Royal Palace is situated. In 1085 Madrid was conquered by the Christians under Alfonso VI and has remained under Castilian rule ever since.

In 2000, the municipality of Madrid has 2.9million inhabitants with an additional 1.5million in the metropolitan area, mainly to the south of the city. It lies 655m above sea level, in the centre of the huge plain called Meseta which extends over most parts of the historic kingdom of Castile, divided

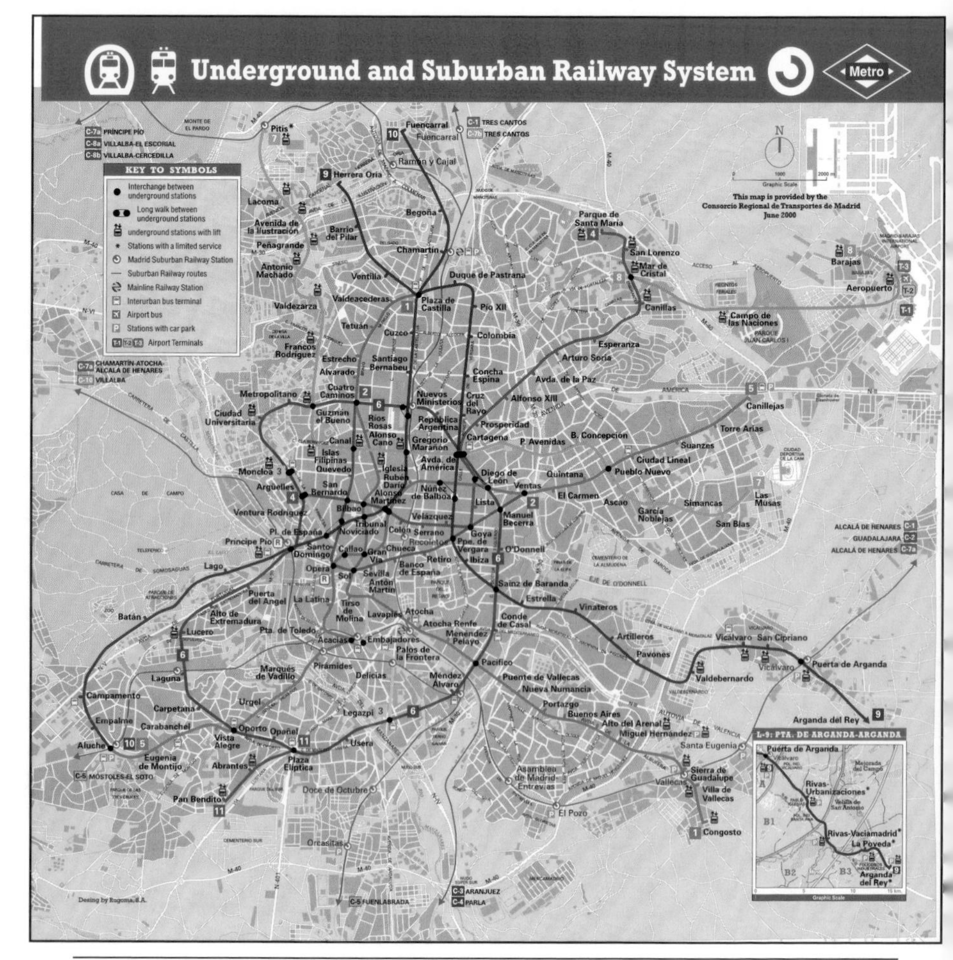

The original diamond shape logo with the name of the station underneath decorates all '*bocas de metro*'.

into two by the Sierra de Guadarrama just north of Madrid. This geographical situation produces a continental climate with very hot summers and quite cold winters. Whereas Castile is now visible on Spain's political map as *Castilla y León* in the north and *Castilla-La Mancha* in the south, the triangle-shaped province of Madrid constitutes a separate political unit called *Comunidad de Madrid,* of which Madrid is the capital.

Similar in size to Rome or Athens, Madrid can definitely boast southern Europe's best rail transport network, one of Europe's oldest metro systems and which is, without doubt, the fastest growing on the continent.

In a few years the underground extension of the Madrid network will make it equal the underground sections in London and Paris (some 188km without counting *Cercanías*, *RER* or *Thameslink* tunnels), this being only beaten by Moscow with approximately 250km of metro underground.

FROM THE BEGINNING TO 1938

In 1870, 22 years after the first Spanish railway started running between Barcelona and Mataró, construction of Madrid's first tramway began. One year later this horse-drawn line started to operate between Puerta del Sol and Salamanca along the streets of Alcalá and Serrano. The network tried to keep up with the growing population, which reached half a million by the end of the century.

In 1892, the first project for five underground lines was presented. Pedro García Faria designed a first line to connect Madrid's three main stations, Delicias, Mediodía (now Atocha) and Norte (now Príncipe Pío) via Puerta del Sol. A second line should have been built from Segovia Bridge to Retiro and the bull ring, also via Sol. He planned a third line from Puerta de Toledo to the hippodrome via Sol. The fourth line was designed as a ring line. He also thought about a new solution to provide electric energy: waterfalls along the Jarama and Manzanares rivers near Madrid. The system was planned not only to transport people but also goods, with a headway of six minutes operating from 08:00 until 01:00. García Faria obtained the necessary concession but the lines were never built.

Between 1898 and 1901 all tramways in the central area of Madrid changed to electrical traction. At that time Manuel Becerra Fernández presented another project for an underground railway, which was meant to connect a ring rail line to the city centre via an underground route using steam locomotives. Both projects had also envisaged the transport of cadavers to outlying cemeteries.

By the end of the nineteenth century some cities in the world had metros operating. The first of them was London which opened its *Metropolitan Railway* as early as 1863 using steam engines. In 1896, Budapest put a tramway line underground which is today's *M1*. The same year Glasgow inaugurated its circle line. Paris opened its first line (10km) between Porte de Vincennes and Porte Maillot in 1900. Berlin joined the metro community in 1902 with a partly elevated and partly underground railway. A similar ring line opened in Hamburg in 1912. Outside Europe, New York and Chicago had built a number of elevated lines before the turn of the century and New York opened its first subway in 1904, seven years after Boston had constructed the first underground section for its streetcar lines (today's Green Line between Boylston and Park Street). The first underground railway in South America opened in Buenos Aires in 1914.

In 1902, King Alfonso XIII introduced a new era in Spain, the constitutional monarchy. In the same year Carlos Mendoza, Miguel Otamendi and Antonio González Echarte started working

Left L–2 NOVICIADO – one of the older stations of the network. Whereas platforms on L–1 were extended in the 1960s from 60m to 90m, L–2, L–3 and L–4 still have only 60m long platforms which only allow the use of 4-car trains.

Right Mosaic mural at ARGÜELLES – The original vestibule dating back to the 1940s (L–3 and L–4) was totally rebuilt when ring line 6 was finished in the early 1990s.
Capital Transport

together, but only 11 years later did they consider the idea of proposing a metro network for Madrid. The city had a population of 600,000 and was growing rapidly especially towards the north. Eleven tramway companies operated a total of more than 200km of lines, many of which radiated from Puerta del Sol, which caused heavy congestion in the city centre's narrow streets.

Miguel Otamendi designed the project for the first metro line which would run from SOL to CUATRO CAMINOS then at the northern edge of the city. The underground route would just be 1–2 metres below street level between CUATRO CAMINOS and GLORIETA DE BILBAO, and from there to SOL under the older parts of the city at 12–20 metres. It would be double track with 1445mm gauge, the same as the existing tramway lines. Maximum gradient would be 4 per cent and minimum radius allowed 90m. All stations would have to be horizontal (60m long) at an average distance of 500m. SOL and CUATRO CAMINOS were expected to attract more passengers and would therefore have 4m wide platforms instead of 2.5m. Tunnels would be large enough to allow 2.4m wide cars and the use of an overhead line for electrical power supply.

In 1914, while the rest of the European continent became involved in the First World War, Otamendi applied for the concession to build and operate a metro network in Madrid. The project included 14km of underground lines on four different routes, with the provision to extend the network in the future to cover the whole city and link all railway stations. At that time, Paris already had a network of 92km of Métro which was partly elevated.

Otamendi's proposed network was similar to today's L–1 to L–4. A north-south line via SOL, an east-west line also via SOL, a branch line off the east-west line along Serrano street, and another line along the 'Boulevards' (today's L–4 between ARGÜELLES and GOYA). The metro would operate from 06:00 until 02:00 with an interval of 3–6 minutes. There would be first and second class cars and the ticket price would be 15 céntimos for second, and 20 céntimos for first class, both including free transfer to the other metro lines. There would be no goods service. Otamendi applied for a concession without subvention from the State, an option which allowed the company to fix their own ticket prices.

The concession was approved on 19 September 1916. Madrid had grown to more than 700,000 inhabitants, of which 260,000 would be within the area served by the proposed metro. Otamendi and his partners had difficulties raising the necessary funds to start construction of the first line. King Alfonso XIII, who had shown great interest in the project, intervened and added a million pesetas to

the 2.5million already gathered. Eventually a capital of 10million pesetas allowed the founding of the company, called *Compañía Metropolitano Alfonso XIII* on 24 January 1917. The city administration was not happy with the concession and claimed a fixed sum for the use of Madrid's subsoil and surface during construction. It also wanted that the metro should be handed over to the Municipality instead of the State after the 99 years concession.

Construction work began on 17 July 1917 and the first line between Cuatro Caminos and Sol should be finished within two years and three months, including a depot at Cuatro Caminos. This was not an easy task with a World War raging in the rest of Europe, which meant lack of construction material and rolling stock. Between Puerta del Sol and Glorieta de Bilbao streets (Montera and Fuencarral) are narrow and traffic was very busy on them, so the tunnel could not be built by an open method. Therefore the *Belgian* method was chosen, later improved to the so called *Madrid* method largely used throughout the metro history until modern tunnelling machines were introduced in the 1990s. The second stretch from Bilbao to Cuatro Caminos could be built along wide streets (Luchana and Santa Engracia) so an open method was chosen similar to the *cut-and-cover* method. At a distance of 6m two parallel 0.95m wide slots were opened and filled with concrete as a support for the tunnel ceiling. The central section of the street was then opened in a vaulted form, covered with plaster and then filled with concrete. Some weeks later after the concrete ceiling had dried the tunnel was excavated underneath. The deeper stations in the city centre were equipped with elevators and a small entrance building. While the building of the tunnel advanced, neither a Spanish nor a foreign company could be found to supply the necessary electrical motors for the trains, so some used 125HP motors had to be bought from the Paris Métro which were later substituted by 110HP motors. Although certain materials for the metro construction had to be imported (copper, bogies, electrical motors), most components were produced in Spain.

Before the first line was opened to the public plans for an extension south to Atocha were published. Prices for soil along the first line grew rapidly and the metro company itself founded a new company dedicated to developing the areas west of Cuatro Caminos (see today's metro station Metropolitano on L–6).

The first metro line was officially inaugurated on 17 October 1919. King Alfonso XIII cut the ribbon at Cuatro Caminos and accompanied Otamendi on the first ride towards Puerta del Sol. It was 4km long and had eight stations: Puerta del Sol, Red de San Luis (now Gran Vía), Hospicio (now

Repainted 2000-train at L–2 ÓPERA station. From here a branch line, which is operated separately, was built to connect the city centre to the former Norte station (now PRÍNCIPE PÍO) down by the Manzanares river.

TRIBUNAL), BILBAO, CHAMBERÍ (closed in 1966), MARTÍNEZ CAMPOS (now IGLESIA), RÍOS ROSAS and CUATRO CAMINOS. Two weeks later, on 31 October 1919, the line opened to the public. Because of the number of people expected on the first day, trains initially ran up and down every 6 minutes without stopping at the intermediate stations which were opened gradually as passengers got used to the new service. On that first day 56,000 people rode on the metro. During the following two months, an average of 43,000 passengers a day travelled on the metro.

The initial success of the line showed that an extension south was the best way to increase ridership – while the level of ridership was as planned, it was thought that a longer line could attract more passengers, including to the original section. The 1.8km stretch from PUERTA DEL Sol to the Atocha railway station (formerly called Estación del Mediodía – South Station) was excavated using the *Madrid* method, only a short stretch near Atocha could be built by an open method. PROGRESO (now TIRSO DE MOLINA) station had been designed for a future branch south which would have been today's southern section of Line 3, but a few years later a new alignment was chosen to create another north-south line. This explains the strange route of the two lines south of PUERTA DEL SOL. The ATOCHA extension opened on 26 December 1921 and also helped to increase earnings on the original section, as longer trips meant higher fares. In that year, elevators were installed at SOL and GRAN VÍA which passengers had to pay for separately. The success of the metro continued with another extension of the first line to PUENTE DE VALLECAS (2.3km, opened 8 May 1923), and the construction of a second line from SOL to VENTAS where a bull ring was built. This section opened on 14 June 1924. On the new line, GOYA was planned to allow transfer to the Boulevard Line (now L–4). The first public pedestrian underpasses were built at BANCO DE ESPAÑA under Alcalá Street, probably a sign of progress in those days, but definitely not very attractive nowadays. In September 1923, the *coup d'état* led by General Primo de Rivera replaced Spain's government by a dictatorship which was to last for eight years.

While the eastern branch of L–2 was inaugurated, construction work proceeded on the route from SOL to QUEVEDO with a branch line down to Estación del Norte (North Station, now PRÍNCIPE PÍO). This was the main station for the company that served most lines in Northern Spain, but as it is situated down by the Manzanares river it was difficult to reach by tram because of the steep road leading down there. This double track but single platform line which uses only 4-car-trains (45m platforms) was put into service on 27 December 1925, together with the SOL – QUEVEDO section of L–2. The metro had become the most popular means of transport in the capital, and in one year it transported more passengers than all Spanish mainline railways together.

In 1927 work on a L–2 extension from QUEVEDO to CUATRO CAMINOS began. This would offer people who have settled in this northern part of the city a direct link to the eastern parts of the city without transfer at SOL, but it would also connect the two lines to facilitate the interchange of rolling stock and the shared use of depots and workshops. At the same time, L–1 grew northwards to TETUÁN (1.85km, three stations), with a provision to extend it further to the village of CHAMARTÍN. This section was opened to the public on 6 March 1929. Six months later also the L–2 extension to CUATRO CAMINOS started revenue service. With an average station distance of 500m on the network so far, this was the longest tunnel between stations with 1.5km until an intermediate station CANAL was added almost 70 years later to allow transfer to L–7.

Design for the fourth line included in the original concession started. The third line was planned to run north-south along Serrano Street. When L–2 east was built, RETIRO station was made to substitute two other planned stations, Independencia and Velázquez. The third line should have branched off L–2 at Independencia, but as this station was not built the whole alignment was unfeasible and was then cancelled. Instead the company asked for a branch to run north from GOYA which could eventually be extended to PROSPERIDAD, an area already densely populated at that time.

In 1930, Madrid had 900,000 inhabitants and city planners wanted Madrid to grow northwards along the Paseo de la Castellana artery. Also Barajas Airport was built at that time (the metro would get there just before the end of the century!).

In 1931, after the coalition of left wing parties won the general elections, they proclaimed the republic which brought a direct consequence for the metro company. The king had to leave the country and the company had to change its name from *COMPAÑÍA METROPOLITANO ALFONSO XIII* to *COMPAÑÍA METROPOLITANO DE MADRID*. Shortly after that the construction of the GOYA – DIEGO DE LEÓN branch started. The first ticket vending machines were installed at SOL and CUATRO CAMINOS, which proved to work very well, so more machines were added in the following years.

On 17 Sept. 1932, the branch to DIEGO DE LEÓN was put into service. This branch was served by every other train coming from CUATRO CAMINOS, whereas the ÓPERA – NORTE branch was and still is operated as an independent shuttle service. In 1934 the city forced the company to tear down the entrance buildings at SOL and SAN BERNARDO. The one at GRAN VÍA survived a couple of years longer. The Transport Ministry offered the metro company the use of the rail tunnel being built under Paseo de la Castellana, popularly called *Tubo de la risa* (Tube of Laughter) because it took decades to finish. The company refused the offer as the areas along the line were not very populated, so a deficit would be guaranteed. However, traffic was very good, especially on L–2 where a 2 minutes headway could be introduced. To increase capacities even further, cars were extended from 11.75 or 12.5m to 14.5m. For safety reasons acoustic signals for closing doors were installed. Construction on today's L–3 from SOL to EMBAJADORES had begun in 1932 but water problems delayed work progress.

The last day of 1935 was a record: 400,000 passengers in one day. In February 1936, the left-wing Frente Popular won the elections again which some generals took as an occasion to organise an uprising which led to the outbreak of the Spanish Civil War in July 1936. On 9 August 1936 the first stretch of today's L–3 from SOL to EMBAJADORES was opened without any celebrations, and five days later the ÓPERA – NORTE shuttle was closed as it was badly patronisied before, and now with Madrid almost cut off from its hinterland, not many passengers came into town on the mainline railways.

L–2 RETIRO serves as a gateway to Madrid's large central park. The leisure activities enjoyed there are shown in some images by Mingote within the station, which also hosts a small art gallery.

The northern section of L–3 from Sol to Argüelles had been approved by the government before the war, but its construction would obviously have to wait for more peaceful times.

For the next three years Madrid suffered a permanent siege by the national forces but the metro kept running almost normally. Ópera station, then called Fermín Galán, was closed at times and the branch between Goya and Diego de León was closed and used as an arsenal. The metro not only transported people but also coffins and cadavers to the eastern cemetery. It became the main refuge for the population during the air raids. Some people who had come to Madrid from the hinterland even established their permanent homes in the metro stations. Iglesia station (meaning Church) was renamed into Sorolla by the Republican city government. For the metro the most significant event during the war years was an explosion in the arsenal in the metro tunnel mentioned above. The tragedy happened on 10 January 1938 and caused many deaths although exact numbers are not known. Despite this fatal accident people kept using the metro to take refuge from air attacks, which had become part of their daily routine.

FROM 1939 TO THE POPULATION BOOM IN THE 1960s

National forces under General Franco eventually conquered Madrid on 28 March 1939 putting an end to almost three years of civil war in that part of Spain. Immediately afterwards purification of staff began and lots of new workers were hired to substitute sacked communists and socialists.

The company and the government wanted to give an image of normality and relaunched at once the project to extend the newest line from Sol to Argüelles, although the neighbourhood served was absolutely destroyed by the war. The line was scheduled to be finished by 1941, although at the same time a lot of effort had to be put into rebuilding damaged sections of the original network. To increase capacities, the programme to lengthen metro carriages from 11.75m to 14.3m continued. Gran Vía station was renamed José Antonio (founder of the *Falange*, the Spanish Fascist Movement), Progreso became Tirso de Molina (a classical Spanish writer) and Príncipe de Vergara became General Mola. For the metro company the new government meant political stability, especially no more strikes, which had become a big economic problem before the war. With this perspective of political and social tranquillity ahead, they returned to the idea of building an underground line along the so called Boulevards, from Argüelles to Goya (the western section of L–4). Meanwhile the

Left Trains are swapped between different small profile lines and therefore carry all possible line maps. As can be seen from the station panel, this is an L–2 train (red ribbon under station name) that has just arrived at its northern terminus. L–10 is currently being rebuilt for use of large profile rolling stock.

Right L–10 Lago – a new 2000-series train is heading for Príncipe Pío, a few months before the tunnel profile was widened in 2000.

city government together with the Spanish government founded a transport authority, the *Junta de Coordinación de Transportes de Madrid,* whose aim it was to solve any transport problems in Madrid. In 1941 all mainline railways using Spanish gauge (1672mm) were nationalised and *RENFE* (*RED NACIONAL DE FERROCARRILES ESPAÑOLES*) was founded.

The northern section of Line 3 opened on 15 July 1941 with four new stations. Soon afterwards the builder of the University Campus, then under construction, asked for an extension of that line to the heart of the campus. However, the metro company could not be convinced, as this extension was not considered to be profitable. Eventually 46 years later L–6 would arrive at CIUDAD UNIVERSITARIA.

In 1942, while the rest of Europe was involved in the Second World War, in Madrid construction of L–4 was rapidly underway, despite the difficulties of getting certain materials from abroad. During that year the metro transported more than 250,000 passengers daily on three lines.

The new line opened for traffic on 23 March 1944 and connected the neighbourhoods of ARGÜELLES and Salamanca, the first east-west route that avoided the historic centre of Madrid. Whereas the first three radial lines converged at PUERTA DEL SOL (also km 0 for all Spanish national roads), this new line offered four interchange stations to the previous lines: to L–3 at ARGÜELLES, to L–1 at BILBAO and to L–2 twice, at SAN BERNARDO and at GOYA. The network had grown to 26km and plans for a southern extension of Line 3 had meanwhile matured.

At the end of 1944, two days before Christmas, the metro beat another record: 1,150,000 people were carried in only one day, which meant 90 per cent of Madrid's population at that time. The same day one year later ridership figures equalled Madrid's population census.

People in southern Madrid organised a demand for the construction of an extension of L–3 to LEGAZPI, so work began in June 1946, just after new tickets had been introduced. Until then tickets had the name of the station printed on where the trip was started. According to the length of the journey a different price had to be paid. Cheap day-return tickets were also sold. Fares were slightly higher on weekends. Now tickets could be bought in advance and had to be stamped when entering the station, so no queueing was necessary anymore.

At the end of the 1940s the metro's lead over other means of transport began to decrease. There were still over 140km of tramway lines but they only carried 180 million passengers a year, few compared to the metro's 330 million in 1949. A serious competitor for the next decades was born. In only a few years the bus had begun operating a network of 60km and would replace many tramway lines during the next years. However, the metro still carried more passengers than all other means of transport together. The busiest stations were SOL, ARGÜELLES, CUATRO CAMINOS, GOYA and ATOCHA. On

Left L–10 Batán – a new 2000-series train arriving from Lago in April 2000. In the future trains will continue straight ahead from here to Alcorcón and MetroSur via a new station called Puerta Batán.

Facing page L–10 Empalme – the section between Aluche and Puerta Batán will be served by L–5 in the future, therefore the blue stripe on top of the station name will become light green.

26 March 1949 the first section of L–3 south went into service, adding another 1.3km to the system. Two more stations were inaugurated: Palos de Moguer (now Palos de la Frontera) and Delicias next to the railway station for trains coming from Portugal and Extremadura. This railway station was closed in the 1970s and is now home to the Railway Museum. Technical problems caused the final section to Legazpi to take two more years to be finished. It opened to the public on 1 March 1951. After successful trials at Sol, several central stations were equipped with ventilation to lower temperatures in the summer. There were plans to extend L–1 by 1km at both ends, from Tetuán to Plaza de Castilla, and from Puente de Vallecas to Palomeras (eventually called Portazgo).

Madrid had grown both in area and in population. After some municipalities (Chamartín, Aravaca, Canillas, Hortaleza, Canillejas, Barajas, El Pardo, Vallecas, Fuencarral and Vicálvaro) were annexed to the capital, its population figure climbed to 1.5 million (600km^2) with 400,000 in the surrounding province. Like everywhere else, cars were the future owners of city streets, pushing aside tramways which were gradually substituted by buses and trolleybuses (in operation until 1966).

In December 1951, the Ministry for Public Works presented an overall plan for transport in Madrid. This plan included for the first time the construction of surface lines, so-called *Suburbanos*. Whereas metros and underground railways in other European and American cities had built long sections of their network elevated or at grade (see London, Paris, Berlin, Hamburg, New York, Chicago, etc.), in Spain the term 'metro' had become synonymous for urban underground railway. A first surface line (though partly underground as well) was planned to run from Chamartín to Plaza de España and south-west to Carabanchel. The western section was considered more urgent, in order to connect those parts of town to the centre which were situated on the other side of the River Manzanares. (Eventually in 1998, with the connection of L–8 and L–10, a through service on this route was established.) The metro together with the *Suburbano* should become the backbone of the mass transit system for the city. *Suburbanos* were obviously cheaper to build, but could not run through densely populated areas, so traffic was expected to be lower. This is why both urban railways should be operated by two different companies. The metro company already made it clear that it was almost impossible to build new lines as long as fares could not be increased. They argued that compared with salaries and average prices in 1922, the ticket price in 1954 would have to be almost three times the current price (45 céntimos) to make the company and new extensions viable. Instead of permitting an increase on fares, the State announced it would pay the construction costs of new lines, while the metro company would have to pay for the infrastructure.

In Spain, the 1950s meant migration to big cities. From Andalusia, Extremadura, Galicia and rural parts of Castile, people moved to areas which were or became heavily industrialised, namely Madrid, Barcelona and the Basque Country in northern Spain. The capital of Spain already had more than 1.7 million inhabitants when the Transport Plan was passed to Parliament. This plan included some 50km of new metro lines and 60km of *Suburbanos*: the above mentioned *Suburbano* line to Carabanchel, another one serving the University campus, a long north-south metro line from Chamartín via Velázquez, Retiro and Legazpi to Carabanchel (now partly covered by L–9 and L–6), a transversal line along the axis formed by Cea Bermúdez and María Molina streets towards Ciudad Lineal (now served by L–7). Priority was given to the L–1 extensions mentioned above, a new line from Puerta de Toledo via Gran Vía to Salamanca (the later L–5), another new line from Argüelles to Cuatro Caminos via Guzmán el Bueno (now covered by L–6), and an extension from Ventas to Ciudad Lineal in the east to serve one of the fastest growing parts of Madrid. The whole plan was laid out for a period of 15–20 years with some 3km of tunnel per year. From then on, stations should be 90m long, instead of 60m so far, to be able to use 6-car trains. Discussion came up once again about a direct metro connection to the University campus. The company still argued that 15,000–20,000 students as potential riders were not enough to build a 3km metro line. In the end they agreed to extend L–3 from Argüelles to Moncloa which acts as a kind of entrance gate to the huge campus.

In 1958, the branch line from Goya to Diego de León, which had been served by alternate L–2 trains, was unified with L–4 which meant an increase in frequency on both former L–2 branches.

In 1960, before the first section of the extension project could be put into service, Madrid had already reached 2.6 million inhabitants. Finally on 4 February 1961 the L–1 extension from Tetuán to Plaza de Castilla opened together with the first (and last) *Suburbano* line from Plaza de España to Carabanchel (now the south-western branch of L–10 and L–5 from Aluche to Carabanchel). The latter was also handed over to the metro company but it had to be operated as a different company. At Plaza de España interchange was provided to L–3 and also to L–2 via a long flight of stairs and escalators to Noviciado station. A 2km long tunnel was built between Plaza de España and Lago to cross under the River Manzanares with a gradient of 4.5 per cent despite the big depth of Plaza de España station (one of the escalators installed there was 21.5m, at the time the longest in Europe). Stations were built with 90m long and 5m wide island platforms for alighting passengers and two 3.5m wide platforms for boarding passengers. This type of station was also planned for future metro stations to improve passenger movement. Campamento and Carabanchel stations lie underground while Lago, Batán and Aluche are in the open air. Distance between stations is significantly higher than on metro lines, namely 2km. The line became popular immediately and became really crowded during festivals being held at Casa de Campo Park.

L–1 had reached the northern end of the Paseo de la Castellana artery (then officially called Avenida del Generalísimo) and should be taken further to the projected Chamartín main station and northwards to Fuencarral (later this route would be covered by a new Line 8, now connected to L–10). At that time lengthening of platforms from 60 to 90 metres on the older section of L–1 had begun and was finished in 1966. This is especially visible at Sol, where platforms do not lie exactly opposite anymore. Chamberí station was closed in May 1966 because it was too near to its neighbouring stations Iglesia (230m) and Bilbao (310m) and platform lengthening was technically not possible as platforms had to be totally horizontal and straight. This is Madrid's only *ghost* station.

L–10 Plaza España – an island and two side platforms were built at some stations along the *Suburbano* to improve passenger flow. The exits at the eastern end of the platforms seen here lead to Noviciado station on L–2 via a series of stairs and escalators.

After the city had grown without any defined guidelines during the 1950s, in 1961 the city council tried to establish a plan for further expansion. This obviously also affected future needs of mass transit. New routes were defined for future metro construction:

1 – from San Blas to Chamartín (now partly realised in L–7, L–9 and L–10);
2 – from Estadio Bernabeu to Peñagrande;
3 – Peñagrande – Chamartín;
4 – Estadio Bernabeu – Canillas;
5 – Plaza de Castilla – Hortaleza;
6 – Manuel Becerra – Carabanchel (now covered by L–6);
7 – Extension of the *Suburbano* from Plaza de España to Paseo de la Castellana (now L–10);
8 – *Suburbano* to Villaverde by transforming a railway track (now served by *Cercanías* C–5).

So Madrid never lacked projects for its metro and some of them even became reality in the next decades, although sometimes adjusted to the needs of the time.

On 2 July 1962, L–1 reached Portazgo, adding another 1.1km to the network (29.5km) and two stations which had already been built for service with 6-car trains. Apart from the new Atocha-*Renfe* station added in 1988, from then on L–1 would remain unchanged until 1994, despite the pressure by the population to carry it 4km further south to Villa de Vallecas. Because the line was already so crowded, in some stations, first at Atocha and Bilbao, platform doors were installed to protect people at the front of the platform from being pushed to the edge by people behind.

On 17 July 1963, L–3 reached Moncloa and thus its full length. Like on L–1, this station was also built 90m long, but the rest of the stations on this line are still 60m long. One year later, on 28 May 1964 another section of the urgent plan opened for traffic: the L–2 extension from Ventas to Ciudad Lineal (3km, four stations). This stretch would eventually be connected to L–5 in 1970.

In 1967 the Government approved another *Extension Plan* which included 55km of new lines to be built in 12 years and which should create a network of 100km, including the existing 43km of metro and *Suburbano*. This meant that 85 per cent of the population would then have a metro station within 400m from their homes. Madrid was then expected to have 4million inhabitants by 1980 and that 25km of metro would be needed for one million people, similar to Paris. The plan basically included five new lines, three north-south routes, one east-west and one ring line. While Madrid had just under 3million inhabitants in 1970, the plan was designed for a city of 6million in 2000 (now in 2000 the city has still or once again 2.9million inhabitants). L–4 should be extended to Prosperidad; L–6 should circle the city from Argüelles to Carabanchel; L–7 should run from Cea Bermúdez (now Islas Filipinas) to San Blas; L–8 should be an important north-south axis along Paseo de la Castellana and south across the Manzanares river to Plaza Elíptica. Two more lines should cover the northern and north-eastern parts of the city. Whereas distance between stations is only 500m in central areas, new extensions into outer areas should have an average of 800m between stations to increase travel speed. Stations should have access at both ends with escalators, and travel-lators where necessary. Interchange with the *RENFE* suburban service should be provided wherever possible. As the reader can see from the map some of these lines were eventually built, others were put aside or modified. The plan itself was revised in 1971 (for example L–1 to VILLA DE VALLECAS, L–3 northwards to Vallehermoso, L–9 to PAVONES and L–8 to Entrevías) and updated in 1974.

In the 1960s, the private car had invaded Madrid's streets which were, of course, not prepared for this. Traffic congestion became a serious problem which was partly solved by building a ring motorway, the M-30. Experts already pointed out that the capacity of one metro line was equivalent to 26 motorway lanes in each direction or to four bus lines running on separate right of way with a 30 second interval.

While lots of plans were made for the future, on 5 June 1968 the first 7km long section of L–5 from CARABANCHEL to CALLAO went into service. Three stations in the older part of town, CALLAO, LA LATINA and PIRÁMIDES were equipped with escalators, for these stations lie 20m deep. The line was not an immediate success, partly because of higher fares compared to the rest of the network.

For the metro's 50th birthday in October 1969, Marino Gómez Santos published a book called *El Metro de Madrid – Medio siglo al servicio de la ciudad. 1919–1969* (Half a century serving the city). The following years would become economically difficult for the company and for the first time nationalisation was proposed. To make services more attractive, tariffs were standardised and a weekly and a monthly pass were introduced. From now on any trip on the metro would cost 3 pesetas (4 for a return ticket). Weekly passes for 20 pesetas included six return trips, monthly passes 25 return trips for 80 pesetas. The first ride had to be done before 09:00 in the morning. The increased fares had a negative effect on total ridership which decreased by 1 per cent the following year, despite the new L–5.

The central stretch (CALLAO – VENTAS, 4.4km, seven stations) of L–5 opened on 2 March 1970. On 20 July 1970 the VENTAS – CIUDAD LINEAL section of L–2 was connected to L–5 creating a 13.9km long line with 22 stations. The entire line could be supervised by only one person from a central control point, a system already operational on L–3.

With the completion of L–5 (which would later be extended to CANILLEJAS) the era of small profile lines came to an end in Madrid. From now on, all new lines would be built following large profile standards.

L–5 ÓPERA – most stations along the southern leg of the line look similar. Here transfer is provided to L–2 and the branch line to PRÍNCIPE PÍO.

1970s and 1980s

The new decade started with an agreement between the metro company and the army, which offered young men the possibility to do their military service with the metro. In previous years services were interrupted several times by labour conflicts. The permanent presence of soldiers would help to avoid these situations. This agreement was in force until 1984.

On 26 March 1973, L–4 grew 2.5km and reached ALFONSO XIII. At AVENIDA DE AMÉRICA interchange to three (!) other metro lines would be provided soon. In spite of this new extension, 1973 was the last year in which the metro company made profits. On 17 July 1974 the first section of a large profile line was inaugurated: L–7 from PUEBLO NUEVO (on L–5) to LAS MUSAS.

In 1974 the metro expansion plan was updated. At that time several sections of new lines were under construction: L–4 from ALFONSO XIII to ARTURO SORIA; L–5 from CIUDAD LINEAL to CANILLEJAS; L–6 CUATRO CAMINOS – OPORTO; L–7 from PUEBLO NUEVO to LAS MUSAS; L–9 BARRIO DEL PILAR – AVENIDA DE AMÉRICA. The revised plan included a L–1 extension from PORTAZGO towards Santa Eugenia (three stations opened in 1994, the rest of the line was later modified to go to CONGOSTO), one more station on L–4 (ESPERANZA, opened in 1979); L–6 as a full circle line via NORTE (now PRÍNCIPE PÍO, 1995); L–7 west from AVENIDA DE AMÉRICA to Cisneros (later modified and opened to ISLAS FILIPINAS and then north in 1999); L–3 to meet L–7 at Cisneros (not realised); L–8 Nudo Norte – NUEVOS MINISTERIOS – ATOCHA and then two branches south, one to Martínez de la Riva parallel to L–1 and another one southwest to PLAZA ELÍPTICA (the northern part opened in 1982, the rest has never been built, although the south-western branch might be part of today's L–11 one day); L–9 from Moratalaz (PAVONES) to AVENIDA DE AMÉRICA (fully completed in 1986), and finally the extension of the *SUBURBANO* (L–10) to ALONSO MARTÍNEZ (finished in 1981).

All new lines had to be built to large profile standards, which meant 115m long platforms instead of the previous 60/90m, larger tunnel sections to allow the use of new rolling stock, the 5000-series which were 18m long and 2.8m wide (the 1000-series on small profile lines is 14m long and 2.4m wide). On L–7 for the first few months 1000-series carriages had to be used due to late arrival of 5000-series stock, so to bridge the gap between platforms and train doors a board had to be fixed to the trains. The second section of L–7 between PUEBLO NUEVO and AVENIDA DE AMÉRICA was put into service on 17 May 1975 (2.8km, five stations), but nonetheless total passenger numbers fell by 3.8 per cent that year. The company did its best to improve the overall service of the network by permanently renovating the infrastructure, by making stations more comfortable in the summer through ventilation on L–5 (a decrease of 6 degrees Celsius) or by installing turnstiles to save ticket checking personnel.

In November 1975, dictator Franco died and a new era began for Spain. For the last few years while the network was growing, the company's deficit also increased more and more which was due to increases in service costs, mainly rising salaries, without parallel fare increases. Passenger numbers had fallen because more people got a free Saturday and worked without a long lunch break during the week. Strikes were another reason for less revenue. This situation caused the State to intervene in 1976, but it would take ten years until the metro became a fully public enterprise. This difficult economic situation also delayed the opening of already built sections (L–4 ARTURO SORIA and L–6 CUATRO CAMINOS – PACÍFICO) which would not begin regular service until 1979.

During 1976 trial runs were made on the new L–7 to introduce the ATP (automatic train protection) and ATO (automatic train operation) systems which are now the standard on all metro lines, except L–2 and L–5. This system allows the train to run automatically after the driver gives the command to leave the station by pressing two buttons. Meanwhile the metro suffered a series of quite serious accidents, which badly damaged the metro's safety reputation.

On 28 October 1976 a new suburban line was opened from ALUCHE to MÓSTOLES. This 13.5km long line was developed from a former narrow gauge line between Madrid and Alvorox. Double track was laid with Spanish gauge as the line was supposed to be operated by *RENFE*. 2.3km were built underground and should be extended to LAGUNA and towards the city centre in the future. To improve interchange with the metro at ALUCHE, L–5 trains would run from then on to this terminus where also *SUBURBANO* (L–10) trains would reverse.

While Spain struggled to become a modern democracy the metro struggled to survive. The deficit kept growing, infrastructure got worse and accidents including fire and derailments and other service disruptions increased. Also vandalism and mugging became a new problem, mainly in some central stations. As a consequence, in June 1978, the State dictated that the company would depend directly on the Ministry of Transport and should be governed by an Intervention Council. Eventually it should become the property of the Municipality of Madrid. The *SUBURBANO*, which although operated by the metro was the property of *FEVE* (Spanish Narrow Gauge Railways), would also be handed over to the city. One of the first measures was to put the already built lines (L–4 and L–6) into service. Although legally the company was still owned by its shareholders a new slogan was coined which prepared for a new era: *Help us renew the Metro. The Metro already belongs to all of Madrid's people*.

In 1979 Madrid voted for a Socialist mayor while the Spanish government was still in the hands of the centre-right UCD. This situation did not help to find a quick solution to the metro's problems.

On 5 January 1979 the L–4 extension from ALFONSO XIII to ESPERANZA finally opened its doors (2.3km, three stations). A long section of the new L–6 appeared on Madrid's metro map on 11 October 1979: CUATRO CAMINOS – PACÍFICO (7.2km, ten stations). This was the first part of what would become Madrid's longest and busiest underground line, finished in 1995. On this section some of Madrid's deepest stations can be found: CUATRO CAMINOS 49m below street level, SAINZ DE BARANDA, 42m. Shortly after, on 18 January 1980 L–5 reached CANILLEJAS (2.9km, three stations) and on 31 January 1980 trains of the 5000-series travelled on the new L–9 from SAINZ DE BARANDA to PAVONES in Moratalaz (3.9km, five stations). The total network had grown to 73.5km and had 114 stations. 28km more were under construction (L–6, L–8 FUENCARRAL – PL. CASTILLA, L–9 and L–10). Together with a series of measures to improve the overall system, a corps of private guards was formed in order to improve passenger safety. A questionnaire was handed out to half a million people to find out exactly what their travelling habits were and to modify the expansion plans once again. Also the tariff system should be revised and improved. It was shown that return tickets and monthly passes were hardly used because of the time restrictions for the user. Finally tickets on offer were reduced to a single ticket (25 pesetas) and a ticket with 10-rides (215 pesetas), which are still the basic tickets in Madrid in 2000 (plus the now very popular Abonos).

The survey carried out showed that a third of all motorised trips were made by metro, another third by bus and the remaining third by private car or taxi. 65 per cent of metro users went to their station on foot. The now fashionable concept of 'Park&Ride' hardly existed then. The new sections opened in the previous years were under-utilised compared to the older lines. Whereas older lines had an index of 5.3million passengers per kilometre these new additions to the network only reached 0.7–2.5. This was partly due to the fact that these lines led to residential areas which create very low traffic in off-peak hours, but also because of the extreme depth of stations and long corridors at interchange stations (and almost everybody had to make at least one transfer to get anywhere). At the same time the older lines running through the city centre suffered from old rolling stock. The new 'Plan for Modernisation and Improvement' tried to find a solution to these problems. Stations should be renovated, new ticket vending machines installed, technical installations improved and new rolling stock should be ordered. The new 2000-series should replace older trains dating back as far as 1919. The newest train running on small profile lines was from 1965. L–1 to L–5 should be equipped with ATP after positive experience on the new lines. This system prevents a train from passing a red signal and controls its speed depending on the location of the previous train and the alignment of the track.

In the summer of 1981 new station panelling was introduced to improve orientation in the growing network. Shops and bars opened in metro vestibules and corridors to create a nicer atmosphere. And in order to co-ordinate all means of transport operating in and around Madrid a transport authority should be created.

On 7 May 1981 the southern section of L–6 reached OPORTO (5.7km) with two interchange stations at LEGAZPI to L–3 and at OPORTO to L–5. At MÉNDEZ ÁLVARO a transfer facility to *CERCANÍAS* would be built in the future. On 18 December 1981 L–10 (the former *SUBURBANO DE CARABANCHEL*) penetrated the centre as far as ALONSO MARTÍNEZ (1.4km) which provided a new interchange with L–1 at TRIBUNAL and with L–4 and L–5 at ALONSO MARTÍNEZ.

In 1982 the Socialists moved in at Moncloa, the headquarters of the Prime Minister, and the

Left L–5 Alonso Martínez – a 1000-series train is still in service in April 2000, but soon all trains of this generation and now only operating on L–5 will be replaced by new 2000-trains currently running on L–10 and L–8, which will use large profile rolling stock in the future.

Right L–5 terminus Aluche – a 1000-series train leaving for Canillejas in April 2000. In the future only new trains will continue to the new terminus at Puerta Batán.

same year the Province of Madrid was converted into one of Spain's Autonomous Regions, creating thus a kind of federal district. The new government approved a Plan for Immediate Action for the metro, which consisted basically of modernising older stations used by 75 per cent of all passengers. The building of new lines would be suspended until the former plan had been thoroughly revised. While production of the 2000-series trains started, new 5000-series trains arrived which had a 'chopper' installed which allows the recuperation of energy. These trains would be operated by only one person which caused a conflict between company and workers. In 1982 the Traffic Control Centre (CTC) at Pacífico was inaugurated. The whole computer network, communication system and all auxiliary equipment of power supply were installed there.

On 10 June 1982 the last of the new lines of the expansion plan opened to the public: L–8 between Fuencarral and Nuevos Ministerios. The line, which is now the northern part of L–10, was 6.3km long and serves the northern main station Chamartín although access from the metro station to the central vestibule is quite a long walk. Among the other stations was Lima which in 1998 was renamed into Santiago Bernabeu, the founder of the Real Madrid Football Club whose stadium is next to this station. The same year Spain hosted the Soccer World Cup. Despite this major event and the new line in operation total passenger numbers kept falling by 2 per cent in 1982. Until then, Estrella on L–9 was the least frequented station but now Cuzco and Lima took the last places in the ranking. This was probably so because the line didn't offer any continuation towards the city centre. 65 per cent of all passengers used a single ticket which then still cost 25 pesetas, the 10-rides ticket went up to 240 pesetas and the 10-rides return to 360 pesetas.

The analysis of the former expansion plan showed that lines were planned not really following the established travelling routes. Stations were too deep and corridors at interchange stations too long and sometimes labyrinthine. No more construction work would be awarded and work in progress on L–6 between Laguna and Puerta del Ángel would be stopped.

On 1 June 1983 the south-eastern section of L–6 opened between Oporto and Laguna (1.6km, two stations). This extension would allow passengers arriving at Laguna on the future underground extension of the Móstoles suburban line to transfer to the ring metro line.

Two days later, on 3 June 1983, the northern end of L–9 started operation between Herrera Oria and Plaza Castilla (four stations). This section included the 100th kilometre of the Madrid metro network. Its continuation to Avenida de América went into service on 30 December the same year and the ten northern stations (7.3km) isolated from the southern section of the line were operated as line 9B for the next two years. For the first time in its history the Madrid metro had too many metro cars in their depots, 80 of the 5000-series would not be used due to low ridership and these cars could not be transferred to the busier older lines because of the different station and tunnel profile there. On some lines 2–3 car trains were operated, on L–8 and L–9 a fixed timetable was introduced instead of intervals. Therefore these lines were nicknamed 'crono-lines'.

While the creation of a single transport authority was progressing in 1984 some reminders of the former political era were erased from the metro map: José Antonio (L–1 and L–5) returned to its original name Gran Vía, General Mola (L–2) would become Príncipe de Vergara. Elvas on L–6 was renamed Opañel.

The railway plan for the metropolitan area defined the importance of the suburban rail network operated by *Renfe* which should be connected to the metro and city buses. A survey carried out by the new Transport Department of the *Comunidad Autónoma de Madrid* showed that almost 50 per cent of all trips in Madrid were done by private car. While the metro transported 1,400,000 and buses 1,600,000 people a day, suburban trains only carried 180,000. Metro and buses together only needed 17 per cent of the overall energy consumption.

In 1985 the first *Intercambiador* (public transport hub) was built at Aluche to facilitate interchange between all different means of transport: metro, suburban rail and local and interurban buses. Also for the first time a TV advert was shown, and a book called *El Metro de Madrid. Gente, colores, gestos* (People, colours and gestures) was published in order to communicate with the public. In March 1985 tourist passes for three and five days were offered for sale. On 16 December 1985 the single transport authority was finally constituted, the *Consorcio Regional de Transportes* was born which comprises the different levels of administration, Madrid city and surrounding municipalities, *Comunidad Autónoma de Madrid* and Spanish State. Apart from these, representa-

L–6 Manuel Becerra – deep 3-platform stations were built along the original eastern section of the Circle line. Although these stations are not so easily accessible, L–6 is the busiest of all lines.

tives of the major transport operators and the consumer associations have a vote. Its function is to plan transport infrastructures and services, programme investments and operation, establish a common tariff system, award and control of concessions and the supervision of public enterprises.

On 24 February 1986 the middle section of L–9 between Avenida de América and Sainz de Baranda opened for traffic (2.8km, three new stations). For the first time travellators were installed in long corridors at interchange stations. With this addition, ridership rose 40 per cent on the whole line.

In March the Municipality and the *Comunidad de Madrid* finally took responsibility of the Metro, but on 31 December 1986 they passed their shares on to the *Consorcio* which became the only owner of the Metro. The *Consorcio* studied the extension of L–8 from Nuevos Ministerios to Avenida de América and of L–6 from Cuatro Caminos to Ciudad Universitaria. The first was put into service on 23 December 1986 and had been built as a single track 1.4km long service tunnel. This fact limited the service provided and its joint operation with L–7, then also terminating at Avenida de América, but at least it improved significantly the transfer options for L–8 passengers (L–4, L–7, L–9). That year on L–3, Palos de Moguer was renamed into Palos de la Frontera, the place where Columbus started his first voyage towards the new world.

The *Consorcio* also started introducing new tickets which had been almost unchanged since the metro's foundation. Together with a fare rise in August, a magnetic 10-ride-ticket was put on sale for 400 pesetas. The single ticket was then 50 pts. Combined tickets with the *Renfe* suburban lines were also offered. At the beginning of the next year, 1987, for the first time an unlimited monthly pass (*Abono Mensual*) valid for buses, metro and suburban lines was introduced. To avoid unnecessary competition between operators some EMT bus routes were redirected. Passengers had to get their personal ID card as the ticket was not transferable and could buy their monthly coupon also at news stands. The entire *Comunidad de Madrid* was divided into three zones, of which Zone A was the city and zones B and C the surrounding areas. The fare system has changed little since then and is explained in detail in the chapter 'Fare System'.

On 13 January 1987 the long awaited extension to the University Campus reached the faculties from the east and not from ARGÜELLES or MONCLOA as was often asked for in the past. CUATRO CAMINOS – CIUDAD UNIVERSITARIA on L–6 is 2.1km long and includes two intermediate stations, GUZMÁN EL BUENO, a very deep station (42m), from 1999 on transfer station to L–7, and METROPOLITANO, a name remembering housing estates built by the metro company decades earlier.

At the end of 1987 the Transport Department of the Regional Government defined the transport strategies for the Madrid region which included selective extensions of the network, basically the completion of the ring line L–6, a southern extension of L–1 to Sardinero-Sandi, a connection of the three radial lines L–7, L–8 and L–10 and new transportation hubs at PLAZA CASTILLA and PRÍNCIPE PÍO (including L–6 and L–10). Meanwhile the suburban Móstoles line (now C–5) crossed under the Manzanares river to reach EMBAJADORES and provide transfer to L–3 and L–5. The 4km long underground section was eventually put into service on 28 May 1989. At the same time Madrid's busiest station Atocha was largely rebuilt which included a new *CERCANÍAS* station parallel to a new main line terminal (the standard European gauge high speed link to Seville, AVE, started operating from here in 1992). The original 19th century station building was converted into a huge green-house which serves as a waiting room for the station complex. For the Metro a new station was added on L–1 to allow better transfer between different modes of rail transport. ATOCHE-*RENFE* was inaugurated on 25 July 1988.

All these efforts by the new *Consorcio* were reflected in a 3.4 per cent rise in passenger numbers in 1987 compared to the previous year which would increase again by 7 per cent the next year to reach a total of 370 million passengers.

In 1989, just before its 70th birthday, the Metro changed its named again, from *COMPAÑÍA METROPOLITANO DE MADRID* to a simpler *METRO DE MADRID*. The network was then 112.5km long and had 155 stations of which 26 were transfer stations between 2–5 lines. Eight stations allowed transfer to *RENFE CERCANÍAS* and one (MÉNDEZ ÁLVARO) was connected to the southern bus terminal. Almost all lines had been equipped with ATP and new extensions (L–1, L–6) were being prepared. A connection to the airport and to the new fair-grounds at CAMPO DE LAS NACIONES was also considered a priority. An extension of the existing lines L–4 or L–5 was studied. Other alternatives made use of an existing rail line from CHAMARTÍN or even a new elevated rail line. All these plans suffered long delays as the city government changed to centre-right wing while the *Comunidad* was still in the hands of the Socialists.

L–1 L–6 PACÍFICO – the former control centre seen here was transferred to a larger office at ALTO DEL ARENAL in July 2000.

At Mar de Cristal a new transfer station was created between the extended small profile line 4 and the new line 8, which provides a fast link from the city centre to the airport.

THE NINETIES

After the last extension of the Madrid Metro to Ciudad Universitaria on L–6 in 1987, a metro station was within reasonable walking distance (600m) for 58 per cent of Madrid's population (65 per cent if *Cercanías* is also considered). On a normal workday the metro was used by 1.5million passengers reaching more than 400million a year in the early 1990s. This increase (3–6 per cent per year) after the dramatic fall in ridership during the 1970s and the first years of the '80s has various reasons. Obviously a good economic situation experienced in that period created more mobility than before. But it was also the *Consorcio's* effort to improve and co-ordinate public transport in the Madrid area by buying new rolling stock and buses (the average age of metro trains was reduced from 21½ years to ten years), by refurbishing stations, renewing security equipment and infrastructure and by introducing the Abono Transportes which gave passengers the freedom of travelling around the network without any restrictions. In 1993, 53 per cent of all trips were made on season tickets. Parallel to the Metro, the *Renfe Cercanías* more than doubled ridership in five years while new trains were gradually introduced through the 1990s.

During the 1980s the area of Palomeras south of Portazgo on L–1 was heavily restructured and new housing developments were carried out. Therefore an extension of L–1 to these areas where some 70,000 people lived was decided upon. Another priority was the completion of the planned circular line L–6 in the west of Madrid. These two extensions formed the Expansion Plan for the Metro 1990–1994 with 9km and 9 new stations.

The extension of L–1 began in 1990. It is 1.4km long and includes three new stations. For the tunnel and the first station, Buenos Aires, the traditional *Madrid* method was used, the other two stations, Alto del Arenal and Miguel Hernández, were built by *cut-and-cover*. The latter also includes a car park on top of the station for 900 cars. All stations are 90m long, the first two have side platforms and the last, Miguel Hernández, has an island and two side platforms. Following new guidelines for accessibility of public places for people with reduced mobility, Alto del Arenal and Miguel Hernández were equipped with elevators. Trains started running on Madrid's extended original metro line in April 1994.

The completion of L–6 was of extreme importance for the whole network as the new line would finally function as a distributor for the other lines and for all *Cercanías* lines. In the west of Madrid the huge Casa de Campo park penetrates the city like a wedge. As it is an unpopulated area and already served by L–10 there was no need to take the ring line through it to form a proper circle. Instead a new interchange station should be built at the former Estación del Norte, now renamed Príncipe Pío, where bus passengers could change to the ring line L–6 to go anywhere in Madrid, to L–10 to go anywhere in central and northern Madrid, or to the branch line R to go to the historic centre of the city. This major transportation hub which incorporates three metro lines and a *Cercanías* station was built by the Spanish Ministry of Public Works together with the so-called Green Corridor (*Pasillo Verde*) from Príncipe Pío to Atocha now used by C–7b and C–10. The section between Laguna and Puerta del Ángel had already been started in the early 1980s but was abandoned in 1984. Between the latter and Príncipe Pío the new line had to cross under the Manzanares river and meet L–10 at Príncipe Pío at the same level to allow cross-platform interchange, the first of this kind in Madrid. The remaining two stations between this one and Ciudad Universitaria in the north would also be interchange stations and according to new guidelines the walking distance between lines should be as short and comfortable as possible. At Argüelles where L–6 meets L–3 and L–4 the existing vestibule was enlarged to improve access and transfer between lines. At Moncloa a new ticket hall was built which also serves for the new underground bus station. The running tunnel between Ciudad Universitaria and Moncloa and the river crossing were executed by the *cut-and-cover* method while the rest was built by the traditional Madrid method or precutting. A short stretch south of Príncipe Pío was excavated by NATM. Argüelles station was also built in a cavern. All stations follow the standards of the large profile lines and are 115m long and have side platforms. Lucero, Príncipe Pío, Moncloa and Ciudad Universitaria were equipped with elevators. The full circle line eventually opened in May 1995. It became Madrid's longest and busiest metro line with 24km and 27 stations and some 500,000 passengers a day. From then on, directions were obviously not shown by the terminus station anymore but by platform 1 (Andén 1 – anti-clockwise) and platform 2 (Andén 2 – clockwise). The construction of this line included two new depots, one at Ciudad Universitaria and the other 1km from Laguna. Apart from L–8 and L–11, in the year 2000 L–6 offers transfer to all other lines twice.

In the meantime, thorough studies were carried out by the *Consorcio Regional de Transportes* which concluded in the Transport Strategies for 2001 presented in 1993. This showed some obvious areas where the expansion of the current metro network would be of priority. The base was that every person should have a metro stop within a 600 m radius, i.e. within 7–8 minutes walking distance. This was true for some 70 per cent of Madrid's population in 1995, including some areas in southern Madrid served by a metro-like *Cercanías* line. In Madrid's city centre within the M–30 motorway, the so-called 'central almond', even 85 per cent of the population had a metro station nearby. The study also showed that about 60 per cent of all trips done by public transport terminate or originate within this central area due to a strong concentration of jobs there, especially in the services sector. On the other hand, Madrid's population is migrating to the outer areas and even outside the city limits. While the total population of Madrid's metropolitan area has remained quite stable since 1960 (approx. 4.5 million), the city's population share has fallen from 87 per cent in 1960 to only 60 per cent in 1991.

The areas where a lack of high capacity public transport was most evident included the north-western areas of Valdezarza and Peñagrande, the north-eastern areas between Chamartín and Esperanza in the district of Hortaleza, new housing estates in the south-east at Valdebernardo and Vicálvaro, and the Carabanchel Alto neighbourhood in the south-west. These deficiencies should mainly be solved by extending existing lines, namely lines L–4, L–7 and L–9, and by building a branch line for Carabanchel. The connection of two radial lines, L–8 and L–10, was considered another important step towards a better network. L–10 should also be extended towards the south-west from Batán to Campamento (a project which finally was not included in the 1995–1999 extension plans, but which is now being built in conjunction with the MetroSur project). These extensions would have increased the 600 m station access rate to 75 per cent of Madrid's population. At the same time the *Renfe Cercanías* service should be improved by adding new stations and constructing new interchange points with the metro. In 1993 a 26km extension was considered necessary to be built in 8 years at a cost of 12,000 million pesetas a year. The L–10 extension to Campamento should have been paid as part of the area development project.

In the spring of 1995 the Spanish central-right wing party *Partido Popular* already ruling the city of Madrid made the extension of the metro one of their main issues during the election campaign for the regional government of the *Comunidad de Madrid*. They promised 20km for the next four years and won with an absolute majority. During the previous legislation period under Socialist rule only about 9km could be inaugurated (L–1 and L–6).

In August 1995 design for an initial 32km of line extensions began, which included the projects mentioned above and another L–1 extension to VALLECAS, a longer new section for L–7 to PITIS, and a new branch line (L–8) to serve the Madrid trade fairgrounds. The final decision did not include the L–10 Campamento extension and the branch from CHAMARTÍN to Hortaleza. One year later the 18km surface line to ARGANDA DEL REY was added, and in 1997 another 5km were included to extend the newly created L–8 to Madrid's airport at Barajas, an extension which was co-financed by European Union cohesion funds. This made a total of 55km to be finished in only four years.

In September 1999, Europe's largest underground extension project (and after Seoul the second largest in the world) to be carried out in the last decades was completed. With the opening of the Airport station on 14 June and the final extension to the adjacent village of BARAJAS on 7 September 1999, Madrid's metro network had grown from its former 120km to 170km, i.e. more than 50km (of which 37 are underground) and 38 new stations (34 underground) were added to the system at a cost without comparison elsewhere in Europe. The total cost of the underground section of the extension amounts to US$1,400million which represents US$37million per kilometre (US$43million including new rolling stock – 226 cars). In comparison the much promoted London Jubilee Line extension, which includes 16km and 11 stations (12.4km and eight stations underground) has a total cost of US$375million per kilometre and took nine years to build. The fully automated Line 14 (Météor) of the Paris Metro (7km and seven new stations) was under construction for eight years and cost US$155million per kilometre. Athens' new lines 2 and 3 are 18km long (11 stations), were only partly inaugurated at the end of 1999 after 12 years of construction and cost more than US$150million per kilometre, and even the 17.5km (18 stations) of new metro lines in Lisbon built in eight years cost almost double (US$69million per km).

The whole execution of the project wouldn't have been possible without a special financing scheme introduced and based on the Catalan model GISA, an organisation that acts as an agent for the Catalan Government to finance and build roads and other infrastructures in Catalonia. For Madrid an existing company called Arpegio was used. The company's shares are owned entirely by Madrid's regional government and it handles all financial matters concerning the metro extension but does not supervise the construction as such. This company, through public administration, owns large areas of land that can be developed thus offering a real guarantee for credits given by private banks. This Spanish method of finance allowed quick handling of finances and an investment in public transport which wouldn't have been possible with the general budget alone (some 14,000million pesetas a year for the Department of Infrastructures of the regional government).

The surface line to Arganda del Rey was financed by a special loan against future fares. It will run under concession for 30 years after which it will become property of the *Comunidad de Madrid*.

The whole design and construction process was directly supervised by nine engineers employed by the Madrid Regional Government (*Comunidad de Madrid*) who were highly experienced in Madrid's special underground conditions. By avoiding major project management firms and consultants a lot of money could be saved.

Above
Arganda del Rey station at the recently opened end of extended Line 9.
Capital Transport

Left
L–6 L–10 Príncipe Pío – a northbound 5000-series train on L–6 offers easy transfer to a 2000-series train on L–10 visible in the background. This station is also served by the shuttle metro to Ópera and by *Cercanías* trains.

Right
L–9 Valdebernardo – only a few of the new stations were decorated with modern artistic elements like this one in the vestibule.

Construction

For the construction of the underground sections (37km) open face methods like NATM, SCL or pre-cutting were excluded because they were considered too dangerous for Madrid's soft soil, mainly consisting of Tertiary clays and sands, and detritus. Accidents had occurred in other cities like Seoul, London, São Paulo and Munich where soil conditions are similar. As safety for both workers and tunnels was the overall priority for the construction project, engineers decided to use mainly tunnel boring machines in order to guarantee total face, wall and crown stability. Some sections (15 per cent) were excavated by the traditional *Madrid* method (also called the *Belgian* method) in which face sections never exceed 5m^2, and by *cut-and-cover* using diaphragm walls (21 per cent).

In only 13 months, six tunnel boring machines (TBMs) excavated 22km of tunnel, all of them carrying Madrid related names: 'La Adelantada' and 'La Chata' (Mitsubishi-NFM, 9.4m diameter), 'Almudena' and 'Paloma' (Herrenknecht, 9.4m), 'Puerta del Sol' (Herrenknecht, 6.7m) and 'Cibeles' (Lovat, 7.4m). One of the Mitsubishi-NFM machines reached a world record on its way to the airport excavating 792m in 31 days (average more than 18 segmental lining rings/day). All tunnels have double track, except the section between MAR DE CRISTAL and CAMPO DE LAS NACIONES, which has single track tunnels. A computer programme was designed to process all data gathered by some 400 exploratory drills along the alignment to determine risk areas and colour-code them green, yellow and red. During construction all relevant zones of Madrid were covered with sensors to measure vibrations and subsidence. At the same time the TBMs sent 64 variables each minute. Any parameter changes would redefine automatically the colour of risk for a certain section and action could be taken immediately.

All stations were built by using the *cut-and-cover* method except GUZMÁN EL BUENO on L–7 which was built in a cavern by the Madrid method. The *cut-and-cover* method was mainly applied on L–11 along Avenida de Abrantes and partly on the connection of former L–8 and L–10 between ALONSO MARTÍNEZ and NUEVOS MINISTERIOS via the new transfer station at GREGORIO MARAÑÓN, where also the classical Madrid method had to be applied for a section that was especially difficult to build, because of the vicinity of the existing *RENFE* (Spanish Rail) north-south tunnel, two sewer tunnels and because water appeared. Also the L–1 extension was built by this method due to harder clays that tend to disintegrate rapidly.

All stations were designed by the same architect and look quite uniform. Although some stations include artistic elements (for example CAMPO DE LAS NACIONES, AEROPUERTO, VALDEBERNARDO) design is rather simple, putting special emphasis on accessibility (all stations are equipped with elevators and escalators) and total visibility thus giving passengers a better feeling of security. Most platforms can be overlooked from the upper ticket barrier level and stations are kept as close as possible to the surface (average 17m, on older L–6 some stations are as deep as 49m!). Signing follows the standard on all lines and is very easy to understand by using mainly pictograms. The lower two meters of the side walls are covered with easy-to-clean enamelled panels in colours that vary from station to station thus helping people to recognise their station immediately.

Line 1

This small profile line was formerly extended from PORTAZGO to MIGUEL HERNÁNDEZ during the previous extension programme and was finished in 1994. Although not initially considered in the plans, the further extension south was included to serve the district of Villa de Vallecas which so far had only been served by one *RENFE CERCANÍAS* station. The district has some 60,000 inhabitants and is still growing.

The new section is 2.8km long and has three new stations. 1.77km were excavated by the classical Madrid method, the last stretch was built by *cut-and-cover*. Starting in the *cul-de-sac* of the former terminus at MIGUEL HERNÁNDEZ, the tunnel has to go deeper to cross under the M-40 ring motorway which already runs in a rift. Then the line runs under an undeveloped area and after 1400m it reaches the first station called SIERRA DE GUADALUPE. One exit allows access to the Universidad Politécnica, another one goes directly to the *RENFE CERCANÍAS* station Vallecas which 500m east of its original location, replaces the old one. A circular entrance hall was built under the four tracks of which two are reserved for *CERCANÍAS* trains (central platform) and the outer two for

L–1 Congosto – spaciousness and visibility were main criteria for all new stations. Platform areas can be overlooked easily from the distribution level.

passing long distance trains. After some 500m the next station is Villa de Vallecas which is the centre of the district. The 3-level station includes a car park for 40 cars. On earlier maps this station was called Sierra de Gador, the square under which it actually lies. From here the line follows Paseo Federico García Lorca and Calle Congosto and after 1050m it reaches its current terminus Congosto, a 2-level station with red side walls and a blue ceiling. From the southern end of the station the line is prepared to be extended further to new housing developments (Ensanche de Vallecas, 3km with three stations).

Construction of this extension started on 15 February 1997 and it opened to the public on 3 March 1999. The whole project includes 18 escalators and 10 elevators, stations are 95–108m long and 23m wide (with a narrower part of 15m on one end). The total cost was 8,900 million pesetas (€54 million). L–1 Plaza de Castilla – Congosto is now 16.5km long.

Line 4

This line is also one of the small profile lines using only 4-car rolling stock as station platforms are only 60m long. The extension executed in the 1995–99 programme was carried out in two stages. In the cul-de-sac of the former terminus at Esperanza a shaft was opened to introduce the tunnelling machine which excavated some 1500m as far as Mar de Cristal. After some 1000m the first station

L–4 L–8 Mar de Cristal – this large station provides transfer between L–4 and the new airport line L–8 which lies below. Above the tracks the round opening can be seen which lets daylight come into the station.
Emiliano Durán

CANILLAS was built 35m wide, 64m long and 18m deep. The second, MAR DE CRISTAL 550m further on, is a huge transfer station following new criteria of accessibility and spaciousness. A round opening in the centre of the roundabout on the surface allows daylight to come into the ticket hall area. The L–4 station is situated 13m deep in a north-south direction and the L–8 station lies underneath almost perpendicularly accessible in both directions by escalators and lifts. A connecting tunnel from L–8 comes in from the right side, 25m to the north of this station. This first section opened on 27 April 1998. The next station, SAN LORENZO, is only 400m away and lies under a narrow street. Therefore it is only 16m wide and 16m deep (names originally considered were Hortaleza and Barranquilla). The final station PARQUE DE SANTA MARÍA is located 570m further (22m wide and 22m deep). From here the tunnelling machine continued for another 516m to create an access to the newly built depot. The second section opened 15 October 1998. The whole new section is 4.3km long and cost 11,000 million pesetas (€66 million). L–4 ARGÜELLES – PARQUE DE SANTA MARÍA is now 13km long.

Line 7

The extension of this line is, of course, the flagship of the whole extension project between 1995 and 1999 as its original length was more than doubled. Before, this was a radial line serving areas in eastern Madrid, but with only one transfer station along its route (PUEBLO NUEVO: L–5) and long

'Almudena', a 9.4m Herrenknecht tunnelling machine, arriving at GUZMÁN EL BUENO on L–7 on its way north. Emiliano Durán

L–7 GUZMÁN EL BUENO – the only station of the 1995–99 extension programme not excavated by *cut-and-cover*, but by the traditional *Madrid* method . Emiliano Durán

Right L–7 ANTONIO MACHADO – a 5000-series train on a test run a few weeks before opening. Due to its vaulted ceiling this station looks more like an early 1990s station on the last section of L–6 than a typical late 1990s multi-level 'box'-station.
Emiliano Durán

Below L–7 VALDEZARZA – a multi–level view from distribution level down to platform level. Although all areas are under video surveillance, this open arrangement gives passengers a greater feeling of safety in the stations.

walking distances to change lines at its terminus at AVENIDA DE AMÉRICA the line was not used enough. It had to be taken further into the 'central almond' and help to better distribute the entire network. Initial planning also included a route via NUEVOS MINISTERIOS (L–10, *RENFE*) and ESTRECHO (L–1) to VALDEZARZA. But finally the other variant was chosen because this way the new line also serves as an important east-west route between lines 4 and 6 in the central area. Coming from AVENIDA DE AMÉRICA it runs through the districts of Salamanca, Chamberí, Moncloa-Aravaca and finally ends in Fuencarral-El Pardo. The three new transfer stations were expected to generate the most passengers (GREGORIO MARAÑÓN 26,000 per day, CANAL 19,000 and GUZMÁN EL BUENO 6,500). The new section runs west under María de Molina street leaving the single track connecting tunnel to NUEVOS MINISTERIOS which was used by former L–8 for some years. This tunnel built by the classical Madrid method is 1km long. The transfer station to L–10, GREGORIO MARAÑÓN, lies west of the crossroads with Madrid's main artery Paseo de la Castellana and is similar to MAR DE CRISTAL: easily accessible with one station on top of the other and platforms connected by escalators in both directions and lifts (L–7 lies below). This first section opened 13 March 1998, two months after L–10 was connected between NUEVOS MINISTERIOS and ALONSO MARTÍNEZ. After this station L–7 follows the streets José Abascal and Cea Bermúdez westwards and finally turns right into GUZMÁN EL BUENO station.

The first station on this segment is ALONSO CANO which, like the following two, has a car park on top of the station built in collaboration with the city council. Then the line crosses under L–1 between RÍOS ROSAS and IGLESIA, but no transfer was made possible here. A little further, CANAL station lies just west of L–2, for which a new station was added between QUEVEDO and CUATRO CAMINOS while operation on the line was kept in service for most of the time.

This section was put into service on 16 October 1998. From between CANAL and ISLAS FILIPINAS as far as ARROYO DEL FRESNO the tunnel was built by tunnelling machines. Under Calle Cea Bermúdez an underground road was built, together with ISLAS FILIPINAS station. GUZMÁN EL BUENO station is not as deep as the one on L–6, which is one of the deepest on the whole network (42m). Both stations form a V angle and are connected by escalators and travelators.

From here on, the line does not follow streets anymore, although stations are located under them, like FRANCO RODRÍGUEZ which lies under Avenida Pablo Iglesias. The next station VALDEZARZA (initially called Virgen de la Paloma) is one of the most architecturally interesting as the shaft built to introduce the tunnelling machine was left open. Also concrete ceilings have wide holes which gives passengers a feeling of spaciousness. The stretch between CANAL and VALDEZARZA started operation on 12 February 1999. The new line continues further north through ANTONIO MACHADO station (at the crossroads of Calle Valderrodrigo and Antonio Machado) and PEÑAGRANDE (under Calle Ganapanes). After crossing AVENIDA DE LA ILUSTRACIÓN trains arrive at the station of the same name, where another car park was built with the station. The next station LACOMA at Plaza Peña Horcajo also has a car park. From here the line runs down under a valley which is being developed and therefore a station, ARROYO DEL FRESNO has already been built, but doesn't yet appear on the official metro map. As the line is not very deep here and the surface is not a built up area the last stretch to PITIS was constructed in a false tunnel.

The terminus station lies parallel to the existing *RENFE CERCANÍAS* tracks. The station is not surrounded by any important neighbourhoods, so it mainly serves as a transfer option for passengers coming in from the north-west on *RENFE CERCANÍAS* trains (C8 and C7a). This last section started service on 29 March 1999. The entire new section of L–7 is 11km long and cost 44,000million pesetas (€265 million). L–7 LAS MUSAS – PITIS is now 19km long.

Line 8

In order to connect the Madrid Fairgrounds (*Recintos Feriales*) by public transport, in 1995 only a branch from MAR DE CRISTAL was included in the 1995–99 extension project after other alternatives had been discussed thoroughly. Amongst them were several routes with an elevated crossing of the M–40 ring motorway, also with an elevated station at CAMPO DE LAS NACIONES. However, these options would have caused too much noise for a neighbourhood already burdened with the motorway. Land expropriation would have been an additional problem. So the choice was for a full underground solution which could have been a real branch line off L–4 to leave from an additional station between ESPERANZA and CANILLAS, but difficult to build. An independent line from CANILLAS was discarded because it would have meant long transfer corridors, due to the location of the planned L–4 station. So finally MAR DE CRISTAL was chosen because it allows easy transfer and is a better option for a future extension of the line into the city of Madrid. The tunnels between MAR DE CRISTAL and CAMPO DE LAS NACIONES are the only ones on the extension project (except some parts on L–10 around PRÍNCIPE PÍO) which are single track tunnels because small profile tunnelling machines were available at the time, one coming from the finished *RENFE* connection between PRÍNCIPE PÍO and ATOCHA (the so-called *Pasillo Verde* – green corridor) and one from Valencia's Metro which had just finished the tunnel between ALAMEDA and AVENIDA DEL CID on L–3 (opened in autumn 1998). CAMPO DE LAS NACIONES station (originally planned as Recintos Feriales) serves the Madrid Fairgrounds which have some 3million visitors a year, the Campo de las Naciones business area which includes hotels, office towers and the Municipal Congress Hall (*Palacio Municipal de Congresos*), and the Parque Juan Carlos I, which is 220 hectares, and hosts different shows in the summer. The station design differs somewhat from other stations of the current extension project. It has a central platform, and side walls are decorated with a long colourful painting showing all different nations and flags (the station's name means Field of Nations). A full metro line was chosen for this route, because only this way could a very irregular stream of passengers be transported. The possibility of adding an intermediate station under the Villa Rosa Park is an option for the future. This first section was opened by King Juan Carlos I and Queen Sofia of Spain on 24 June 1998.

Although originally planned to continue towards the airport, the decision was not taken until 1997 after years of discussion of other possible airport rail links which were: a *RENFE* line from CHAMARTÍN; a *RENFE* branch from the existing Alcalá de Henares route, or a metro extension of either

L–5 or L–7. Finally the choice was for the new Line 8, which will allow a quick direct service to the centre in the future. Two options were discussed: a northern approach via the village of Barajas and then to the terminal area, or a southern approach which arrives at the airport first and then continues to the village. The second route was chosen because it allows future extension to the planned *Ciudad Aeroportuaria* (Airport City) and to the new terminals being built further north. Aeropuerto station is decorated with a huge mural which shows a bird's-eye view of Madrid's central area by night and is located near the terminal for domestic flights, but also connected to the other terminals via travelators. The airport station was opened on 14 June 1999, and the BARAJAS station (originally shown as Barajas Pueblo) was inaugurated on 7 September 1999, the last of the whole project. It is situated on the western edge of the village to serve both the village and the new developments next to Avenida Logroño. With this extension the airport can be reached from practically anywhere in Madrid for less than one Euro, and the Fairgrounds are easily accessible for visitors both from Madrid and from outside arriving by plane.

Above L–8 AEROPUERTO – a bird's-eye view of Madrid's centre as seen from a plane by night welcomes the newly arrived visitors when they enter the airport station. Platform walls are also decorated with aviation related images.

Right L–8 CAMPO DE LAS NACIONES – a large mural on both sides illustrates the different nations of the world. The station serves the congress centre and fairgrounds above, meeting place of cultures and businessmen.
Capital Transport

Until an extension to NUEVOS MINISTERIOS is built to connect the line physically to another large profile line, trains used on this line are of the small profile type (2000-series) which are equipped with special luggage racks. Station platforms therefore are provisionally widened to fill the gap between the platform and the narrow 2000-series trains. MAR DE CRISTAL and CAMPO DE LAS NACIONES stations have airport information panels showing delays, check-in desks, arrivals, etc. Once the line reaches NUEVOS MINISTERIOS, check-in will be possible there, so passengers can get rid of their luggage and travel without their heavy bags to the airport. There are, nonetheless, long-term plans (2015–2020) to build a new airport south-east of Madrid at Campo Real. The airport express metro could then be transformed into a normal metro line by building more intermediate stations. At the time of writing only one intermediate station is being built between MAR DE CRISTAL and NUEVOS MINISTERIOS, a transfer station at COLOMBIA on L–9. The entire L–8 is 8.2km long and cost 24,283million pesetas (€146million), partly financed by EU funds.

Line 9

The extension of this line consists of two very different sections, the underground urban section between PAVONES and PUERTA DE ARGANDA, and the suburban surface section to ARGANDA DEL REY. The first part is 4.6km long and has four new stations and mainly serves the district of Vicálvaro in the south-east of Madrid. Leaving the former terminus PAVONES, the line passes under the M–40 ring motorway and then turns left into the first station (after 1300m), VALDEBERNARDO, which is situated right in the middle of a quite new residential area of the same name. Unlike the next three stations, this one does not have a car park incorporated, so the station looks very high and spacious (15m below street level). Both entrance halls on either side of the station have been decorated with modern sculptures.

After another 1245m and a turn to the right, trains arrive at the next stop called VICÁLVARO, although initially planned as Universidad Ramón Carande, a private university mainly served by this station which includes parking facilities for 100 cars. Platforms are 18m below street level.

The next stop is only 400m away (although 25m deep) and lies in the heart of the old Vicálvaro. It is named after the street under which it is situated, SAN CIPRIANO (at the crossroads with Calle Jardín de la Duquesa) and incorporates a car park for 150 cars. Due to houses very close to the station alignment, part of the station was excavated by the classical method.

The fourth station PUERTA DE ARGANDA (Arganda Gate) is another interchange station with the *RENFE CERCANÍAS* line to Alcalá de Henares and Guadalajara (C1, C2, C7a). It is located some 550m

L–9 – a repainted 5000-series train returning to the city from ARGANDA DEL REY in May 1999. This part of L–9, now operated separately, has a rather suburban character with only four stations along the 18km long route, although more stations are planned as towns keep growing.

Right All new stations are fully accessible by lifts, from street level to the ticket barrier level, and from there down to the platforms. This one is at Campo de las Naciones on L–8.

Far right Access to Gregorio Marañón station (L–7 and L–10) on Paseo de la Castellana. Although all new stations have lifts down from street level, only few stations have escalators between ticket barrier level and street level.

after the previous and lies perpendicularly under the *Renfe* tracks 13m below street level. There is a common ticket office area between the elevated *Renfe* tracks and the underground metro platforms. The metro station has a special alignment as it is used as a terminal station for some trains on this line that do not continue to Arganda del Rey. There is an oval island platform and a side platform in the outbound direction. Trains terminating here change track before entering the station and drop off passengers on the inbound central platforms. Those who want to continue can wait on the same platform for the next train to run through to Arganda del Rey.

The tunnel section was excavated by tunnelling machines (9.3m diameter). Another 670m before trains see the daylight was dug by the *Madrid* method because of very low depth (less than 5m). The whole new tunnel section of this line follows standards for large profile trains (5000-series): minimum radius 250m, maximum gradient of 4 per cent, maximum speed 70km/h. Construction work started in July 1996 and the inauguration took place on 1 December 1998. The total cost was 13.157 million pesetas (€80 million).

Apart from some kilometres of L–5 and L–10 between Eugenia de Montijo and Lago in the south-west of Madrid the entire network is underground. With the extension of L–9 to Arganda del Rey a new surface section with a more suburban character was added to the system. For the first time the Madrid metro leaves the city limits following a former freight line which was totally rebuilt (special fares are applicable according to the zonal system used outside the City of Madrid). This 18km surface extension has only four stations (the terminus at Arganda del Rey was built underground in a false tunnel), but more stations may be added as new areas are being developed. In the beginning about every fourth train (basic 12 minutes headway) continued from Puerta de Arganda to Arganda del Rey to provide service for some 30,000 people living within a 600m radius, but now this section of the line is operated separately by 3-car trains with a denser interval. The new stations are expected to generate 5.6million passengers per year. In the mid-90s the total population of the municipalities through which the new line runs was 50,000, which will seem to increase to 90,000 in the year 2000 and then double until 2010.

Construction of this surface line was paid by a special loan against future fares. A 30-year concession was given to TFM (*Transportes Ferroviarios de Madrid*), a consortium formed by *Metro de Madrid*, FCC (*Fomento de Construcciones y Contratas*), OCP, and the Cubiertas-Entrecanales Group. The total cost of 18,850million pesetas (€113million) was mainly financed by Caja de Madrid. After the 30-year concession period the line will become property of the *Comunidad de Madrid*.

Stations along the line all have parking facilities next to the station (more than 1000 places). Coming from Puerta de Arganda one or two stations might be added in the future within the district of Vicálvaro. The first station Rivas-Urbanizaciones lies in a cut and is totally covered. Also the northern access to the station is now being covered. Another station is planned at Rivas-Centro half way to the next station RIVAS-VACIAMADRID, which like LA POVEDA, lies at grade with a roof that covers 60 per cent of the 115m long platforms, but which is open in the middle. As said before, the terminus station ARGANDA DEL REY is approached through a false tunnel. This station, like RIVAS-URBANIZACIONES, has a round ticket hall with a flat roof at street level.

Construction of this L–9 extension started in April 1997 and opened for regular passenger service on 7 April 1999. It is part of Madrid's longest metro line – 38km HERRERA ORIA – ARGANDA DEL REY. New trains (6000-series) were bought for operation on the new line but also older refitted 5000 trains are used. The new trains have a maximum speed of 110km/h and are the first in Madrid of the walk-through type, though only two cars are coupled like this.

Line 10

The first project of the expansion programme 1995–99 concerning L–10 was the new alignment between LAGO and PLAZA DE ESPAÑA, in order to increase the transfer options in the city centre. In the previous period and together with the completion of ring L–6 a new multimodal interchange station was built at PRÍNCIPE PÍO by the Spanish State, together with a new rail link from this station (formerly called Estación del Norte) to ATOCHA via the so-called *Pasillo Verde* (green corridor). At the same time the regular long distance rail service to north-eastern Spain was transferred to *CHAMARTÍN*. Although existing in other European metro networks such as Munich, Vienna and Stockholm, this is the only station with cross-platform transfer in Madrid. L–6 tracks are situated in the middle and L–10 tracks were planned to embrace the two island platforms thus allowing fast changing between trains in the same direction. To make this possible it was necessary to abandon the 2km long L–10 tunnel between LAGO and PLAZA DE ESPAÑA, and to build two single track tunnels under the Manzanares river and the M-30 motorway. An elevated river crossing was also discussed as the tunnel variant needed very steep gradients. The two single-track tunnels between LAGO and PRÍNCIPE PÍO (about 800m) were excavated by a Lovat 7.4m diameter tunnel boring machine, although the crossing under L–6 had to be carried out manually. This section was finished in 17 months starting in March 1995. The second section between PRÍNCIPE PÍO and PLAZA DE ESPAÑA (820m) started four months later in July 1995, and was excavated by the *Madrid* and the *German* method. Leaving PRÍNCIPE PÍO station on the outer platforms the line runs through a single track tunnel for about 350m until the northern tunnel crosses under L–6, then the two tunnels merge and with a 4.09 per cent gradient trains arrive at PLAZA DE ESPAÑA, which lies 24m higher than PRÍNCIPE PÍO. Service on

L–10 EMPALME showing a red train arriving from BATÁN. FROM 2003 this station will be served by L–5 trains as L–10 will continue further south to Alcorcón thus providing a direct metro link to the MetroSur ring line (L–12) now under construction.

the existing L–10 between ALUCHE and ALONSO MARTÍNEZ was only interrupted for the last six months before the opening date of the whole section on 26 December 1996.

The second project on L–10 was its connection to the former L–8, which operated between FUENCARRAL and AVENIDA DE AMÉRICA and which like other radial lines was not used enough. In 1990, L–8 was only used by 45,000 passengers/day in each direction, L–10 by some 65,000 per day in each direction. The connection of both lines created a new important cross-city line which is now 18km long and offers transfer to virtually all other metro lines (except the branch lines L–8 and L–11) and most *CERCANÍAS* lines. It is expected to transport more than 300,000 passengers per day, which means an increase of more than 50 per cent. Construction work started on 30 April 1996 and was commissioned on 22 January 1998 after 20 months of work which was especially difficult along Paseo de la Castellana, Madrid's main artery under which a railway tunnel connecting Madrid's main stations CHAMARTÍN and ATOCHA already exists. There are also two sewer tunnels and the new metro tunnel had to be built between them at a distance of 1–3m only. The presence of water along the route was another difficulty. Therefore the use of tunnelling machines was discarded in this case and the tunnel was excavated by the Madrid method. Between the two existing stations at NUEVOS MINISTERIOS and ALONSO MARTÍNEZ a new station had to be built together with L–7, called GREGORIO MARAÑÓN. As described above, the L–7 tunnel crosses under the L–10 tunnel and stations lie perpendicularly to each other in an L shape with platforms connected by escalators, stairs and lifts. Initial plans included an independent station for L–7 which, according to calculations carried out by the *Consorcio Regional de Transportes*, would have meant 4000km of walking per day for the estimated 100,000 users of this station. Fortunately these factors have been kept strongly in mind during the whole extension project. The station is situated under Calle Miguel Ángel and was built by *cut-and-cover*. At the southern end the new tunnel starts in the *cul-de-sac* of the former terminus at ALONSO MARTÍNEZ which was some 300m long under Calle Almagro. Between 1990 and 1996, the former L–8 used a single track tunnel between NUEVOS MINISTERIOS and AVENIDA DE AMÉRICA to improve its transfer options (L–4, L–7, L–9). The first 170m coming from NUEVOS MINISTERIOS was double track and was used to connect the new L–10 tunnel. The entire new section is 1670m long.

On L–10 the new tunnels are prepared to be used by large profile rolling stock, although until a remaining section between ALONSO MARTÍNEZ and PLAZA DE ESPAÑA is enlarged, only trains of the 2000-series can be used. Therefore platforms of the former L–8 between NUEVOS MINISTERIOS and FUENCARRAL had to be provisionally widened to fill the gap between platforms and small profile trains.

Line 11

The new L–11 is just a short stretch of what will be an important north-south line in the future. Studies in the early 1990s showed that the area of Carabanchel Alto badly needed public mass transport. Two alternatives had been discussed, one starting at OPORTO, which would have provided transfer facilities to both lines L–5 and L–6. The other, which was the one chosen, provides a better future option of an extension into the city centre towards ATOCHA, basically a route along Paseo de Santa María de la Cabeza which was included as a south-western branch of the original L–8 back in the 1970s. At the other end there are also plans to extend the line further into the district of Carabanchel (Rafael Finat). Meanwhile the line operates as a feeder for ring L–6 and some 50,000 passengers are expected every day, 83 per cent of which will continue their trip on L–6.

The new line is physically connected to L–6 via a 280m long service tunnel (between OPAÑEL and PLAZA ELÍPTICA stations). The new tunnel starts under Paseo de Santa María and crosses over L–6 before the first station PLAZA ELÍPTICA. The two stations are connected via a 130m long foot tunnel. The line then follows Avenida Lusitana and after an S-curve continues along Avenida Abrantes, until after some 800m it reaches the next station called ABRANTES which has exits at both ends of the station. From here the line keeps running straight on and after 700m trains arrive at the final station PAN BENDITO which also has two exits, at either end of the station. Unlike other lines this line was mainly built by *cut-and-cover* all along its alignment (except a 150m long stretch between PLAZA ELÍPTICA and ABRANTES which was excavated by the *Madrid* method). After PAN BENDITO the tunnel continues in a right bend for approximately 200m.

The entire line is 2.2km long and cost 6,720 million pesetas (€40million). Construction work started on 15 February 1997 and the line was opened for passenger service on 16 November 1998.

OPERATION AND FARE SYSTEM

Madrid's metro operates from 06:00 until 01:30. In May 2000 service was extended until 02:30 on weekends and discussions are going on as to whether trains should run all night. During morning rush hours (07:30 – 09:30) most lines run every 2–3 minutes, L–3 having the densest headway of only 90 seconds. L–8 and L–11 operate every 4½ minutes also during rush hours. During the rest of the day, intervals are between 4 and 6 minutes, with a train every 15 minutes after midnight. The shuttle service between PRÍNCIPE PÍO and ÓPERA (Line R) offers a train every 4–5 minutes. Frequencies on all lines are reduced on Sundays and in August, when many people leave the city for their vacation. For some years station panels showed the time elapsed since the last train had passed. New panels show the time remaining for the next train to arrive.

The fare system valid for the Madrid metro and all other means of transport in and around the city is quite simple. The entire province of Madrid (which corresponds to the autonomous region of Madrid) is divided into six ring zones, with Zone A covering the municipality of Madrid and zones B1–B3 the metropolitan area. C1–C2 extend to rather rural areas. There are only three different tickets for the metro, a single ticket, a 10-rides ticket and a monthly travelcard. Although the price for one trip on a 10-rides ticket is not expensive, for visitors it would be very practical to introduce a 1-day or 3-days travelcard. Compared to other Spanish metro cities, Madrid's public transport is very cheap. Prices shown here are for 2000 and in € Euros:

1. *Billete sencillo* (single ticket without transfer) €0.81
2. *Metrobús* (10 rides on the metro or city bus) €4.24
3. *Abono Transportes Mensual* (monthly travelcard):

Zone A	€27.83	(€306 for a one year pass)
Zones A+B1	€32.25	
Zones A+B1+B2	€36.86	
Zones A+B1+B2+B3	€41.44	

For young people under 21 years old a 30 per cent discount is applicable, elderly persons over 65 pay a flat monthly fare of only €7.83 (or €86.14 a year) for all zones within the province. As a consequence of this fare system, 60 per cent of all metro passengers ride on a monthly pass, 36 per cent use the *Metrobús* ticket and only 4 per cent buy a single ticket. Among people travelling on a *RENFE CERCANÍAS* train the rate of season ticket holders reaches 67.5 per cent, as most of these passengers use another means of transport either within Madrid or from the suburban station to their homes. Although single and *Metrobús* tickets are not valid on *CERCANÍAS* trains, prices for this suburban service are very similar.

The L–9 section between PUERTA DE ARGANDA and ARGANDA DEL REY is the only metro line leaving the city boundaries so far. Therefore flat fare single and *Metrobús* tickets are not valid here. As ridership expectations have not been met on this suburban line, a reduction of fares is being

L–4 CANILLAS – all stations have at least one manned ticket office which is also equipped with video monitors to react to incidents in the station as quickly as possible.

Entrance gates at L–2 and L–5 at VENTAS. Tickets have to be introduced only on the way in, as all of Madrid's metro network (except L–9 PUERTA DE ARGANDA to ARGANDA DEL REY) lies within the central fare zone.

L–1 at VILLA DE VALLECAS – inside the ticket office. Video cameras are controlled from the new main control centre at Alto del Arenal, but also from local points.
Emiliano Durán

discussed. When *METROSUR* opens in 2003 the whole fare zone system based on radial lines might be reconsidered.

When the *Consorcio de Transportes* introduced the *Abono Transportes* in 1987, Madrid was the first Spanish city to use magnetic strip cards. The format chosen then is much smaller than the credit card size tickets now popular in the other Spanish, and also in many other European, metro cities. Tickets can be bought from ticket vending machines or from ticket booths. They have to be introduced into validating machines only when entering the system.

In 1998, Madrid's metro transported 437 million people. The new extensions inaugurated during 1999 helped to reach the 500million mark (an almost 20 per cent increase since 1996). *CERCANÍAS* added approximately 150million passengers (in the entire metropolitan area). Public transport has not only become more attractive through new metro lines, but also due to the so-called *Intercambiadores*, transfer stations where metro, *CERCANÍAS* and suburban buses offer easy interchange between different means of transport (like those built at MONCLOA, PRÍNCIPE PÍO or AVENIDA DE AMÉRICA). The success of these stations is also visible in access statistics which are led by MONCLOA, followed by SOL, PLAZA CASTILLA, ATOCHA-*RENFE* and PRÍNCIPE PÍO. Of all metro lines, L-6 is the busiest carrying some 100million passengers a year, followed by L–1 with 90million. L-9 and L-10 experienced an increase of 18 per cent from 1998 to 1999 after inaugurating important extensions. The most spectacular rise in ridership was on L–7 which doubled its length but also its number of passengers from only 13 million to 27 million in 1999.

Out of all Spanish cities, Madrid offers the best transport maps published by the *Consorcio de Transportes*. A pocket-size metro map or a bus map for the central area are available for free at information points or in tourist offices. Larger maps covering the whole city area, certain districts or towns or the entire province can be bought at newsagents or at the *Consorcio's* head office. The metro company distributes its own diagram network map available at all ticket booths.

MADRID CERCANÍAS

Spain's national railway company, *Renfe*, operates an extensive network of suburban railways in and around Madrid. The total length of the system is 279km with 78 stations – 29 of them lie within fare Zone A (basically the city of Madrid) and 14 stations are directly connected to the metro. Most routes are operated in shared traffic with regional, long distance and freight trains. Line C–9 serving the mountainous area of the Sierra de Guadarrama is only single track and has narrow gauge whereas the rest of the network is double track and has 1672mm Spanish gauge. A fleet of 649 cars, of which 120 are double deckers (450-series), operate on ten lines which radiate in all directions from the main station Atocha. On some routes, especially along the city tunnel between Atocha and Chamartín, various lines are bundled and offer a train every few minutes. Line C–5 from Móstoles-El Soto via Alcorcón, Aluche to Atocha and then south to Fuenlabrada via Leganés runs independently from the rest of the lines (42km). It is the busiest of all *Cercanías* lines and could actually be considered a metro line. It is operated in ATO mode with trains every 3½ minutes during rush hours. It runs underground between Las Águilas and Atocha and is partly covered between Méndez Álvaro and Villaverde Alto. It connects to the metro at Aluche (L–5, L–10), Laguna (L–6), Embajadores (L–3, L–5), Atocha (L–1) and Méndez Álvaro (L–6). In the future five more stations will offer transfer to *MetroSur* and L–10.

After new rolling stock (447- and 450-series) had been bought from CAF in the early 1990s, ridership increased by 13 per cent between 1994 and 1999 to 730,000 passengers on a normal workday. Almost 50 per cent of these travel on C–5, the rest is distributed among the other lines, with some 170,000 passengers on the route to Alcalá de Henares (C–1, C–2, C7a), 120,000 on the northwestern corridor to Villalba (C–8, C–10), 67,000 south to Parla (C–4), 45,000 on the northern route to Tres Cantos (C–1, C–7b) and finally only 30,000 on C–3 to Aranjuez. The same type of rolling stock is in operation in other Spanish cities although double-deck trains are only used in Barcelona.

Príncipe Pío – A repainted older 2000-series train on Line R, which provides a quick link between this new transportation hub (L–6, L–10, Cercanías) and from the old city centre (Ópera).

Facing page Atocha – all suburban lines converge at Madrid's largest and busiest station, which is also the terminus for all long distance trains serving southern Spain.

MADRID METRO – Rolling stock

In the year 2000, a total of 1,322 metro cars run on Madrid's 171km network: 940 of them are motor cars and the remaining 382 are trailers. The average age of all cars is 12 years. All metro lines are electrified at 600V and use overhead power collection, with a track gauge of 1445 mm.

Metro cars can be divided into five types:

1000-series (small profile)

These cars are the reminders of a distant past, and were bought between 1965 and 1973. Although they have been refitted they lack the comfort newer rolling stock offers, especially air-conditioning. 131 motor cars and 17 trailers of this series still operating on L–5 will be withdrawn in the next few years as new trains are acquired for L–8 and L–10.

300-series (small profile)

These trains were originally bought between 1976 and 1982 for service on the former Suburbano (now L–10) between Alonso Martínez and Aluche. The 40 motor cars and eight trailers are still in operation on L–5. These trains will also be substituted by the 2000-series by 2003.

2000-series (small profile)

This is the common rolling stock now on all small profile lines (L1–L5, R – width 2.3m). The first of the 349 motor cars and 337 trailers started service in 1984 and gradually all older trains were substituted by these cars built by CAF. The first trains arrived in a pale grey livery with orange doors, but later red was chosen as the basic colour with white doors which carry a red diamond, the symbol of the metro. Recently many of these trains have been repainted in white with blue stripes to match the latest colour scheme.

Above Interior of a 1000-series second generation train, now in use only on L–5. Capital Transport

Left Inside a metro car of the 2000-series. These carriages are only 2.3m wide, and with only 4-car trains on some older lines, capacity is limited.

In 1998, a new generation of the 2000-series was incorporated. These trains were equipped with the newest technology and security systems and changed the image of Madrid's metro cars through their futuristic helicopter-like glass front (therefore they were nicknamed *'burbujas'* which means 'bubbles') and blue and white livery. The interior of the cars is very similar to that of their predecessor. Most of these new cars now operate on L–8 and L–10, but both lines will use large profile rolling stock from 2002 on, when L–8 will have reached Nuevos Ministerios and thus be connected to the rest of the large profile network, and when L–10 will be fully adapted to large profile along its older stretch between Alonso Martínez and Batán. These 2000-series cars will then be transferred to L–5.

Above The motor-car of a mid-1990s 2000-series train. Capital Transport

Right A 2000-series carriage being delivered from CAF's Zaragoza plant in early 1998. Due to their glass front they were nicknamed 'bubbles'. The interior can hardly be distinguished from its predecessor model. J.A. Lapeña

Left An original 5000-series unit in service at GREGORIO MARAÑÓN on the first large profile line. These new lines were built in the outskirts of the city and only showed high demand during peak hours until they were recently linked to the city centre.

Below Mixed liveries on a 5000-series train, the latest style being the white and blue.
Capital Transport

Right Interior of a 5000-series first generation car, with its rather austere look incorporating bare metal and wood grained effect plastic laminate.
Capital Transport

Below Third generation (early 1990s) 5000-series train interior. Changes include the hand rails, ceiling profile and end door design.
Capital Transport

5000-series (large profile)

There are 332 motor cars and 20 trailers of this type designed for operation on the newer large profile network (L6, L7, L9 – width 2.8 m). The first trains began running in 1974 and the average age today is 15 years. There are actually three generations of these trains which can be distinguished by different front ends and interiors. Most trains were delivered in dark and light blue, but some trains carry a red livery. Like those of the 2000-series, some trains have been repainted recently in white and blue.

Above One of the first 6000-series trains on L–7 in 1999. This is Madrid's first attempt to offer a free passage between cars, although this is only possible between two adjacent cars forming one unit. Emiliano Durán

Left Interior view of the 6000-series showing the generous provision of handrails.
Capital Transport

6000-series (large profile)

This is the newest rolling stock in Madrid at the moment. These 88 large profile motor cars were bought from CAF and from Alstom to operate on the extended L–9 at a maximum speed of 110km/h. So far this is the only type of metro car in Madrid in which passengers can move between two adjacent cars (length 36m). They were designed similarly to new 2000-series cars, but instead of the glass driver's cabin they have a rather aerodynamic front.

7000/8000-series (large profile)

In early 2000, 280 new cars of the 7000-series were ordered to be ready for service in 2002–03. Ten 3-car trains will run on L–8 from Nuevos Ministerios to the airport, thirty 6-car trains are destined for L–10 which will then run from Fuencarral in the north through the heart of the city to Alcorcón in the south (24km) and thirty-five 3-car trains will operate on the *MetroSur* ring line. A consortium of CAF, Alstom, Siemens and Adtranz will produce trains for L–8 and *MetroSur*, while those for L–10 will be made in Italy by Ansaldo-Breda. All trains will be so-called *gusanos* (worms) or 'BOAs' which allow passengers to walk through from one end to the other. The total order is worth €330million.

CURRENT AND FUTURE EXPANSION

MetroSur and L–10, L–8, L–1 Extensions

After the spectacular expansion of the metro network during the 1990s, people in many parts of the city claimed an extension also towards their neighbourhood. With 56km of new metro just finished, the Madrid regional government had a difficult task to continue the pace of construction. Therefore everybody was quite surprised when in early 1999 the construction of the so-called *MetroSur* was announced. This new ring line will be 40.7km long and include 27 stations (four more may be built later when needed). It will mainly serve five municipalities south of Madrid: Alcorcón, Móstoles, Fuenlabrada, Getafe and Leganés, which together have a population of almost one million (1.3 million expected for 2020, including the towns of Parla and Pinto). The *MetroSur* ring line will provide transfer to the *Renfe Cercanías* at six stations. It will also serve the University Campus Carlos III at Getafe and Leganés, and the new University Rey Juan Carlos I spread out in various campuses in Alcorcón, Móstoles and Fuenlabrada. 140,000 daily passengers are expected. In the year 2000, 56 per cent of all trips in the area were done by car, which was the highest rate in the Madrid metropolitan area. This rate was still higher for trips between these towns, whereas most trips into Madrid were done by public transport, mainly by train. The *Renfe* C–5 line (Móstoles – Atocha – Fuenlabrada) transports more than 300,000 passengers a day.

This new line as first announced was not connected to the rest of the metro lines. It was basically designed to serve as a feeder for the *Renfe Cercanías* lines running into Madrid. Then the old project of extending L–10 southwards was rediscovered, and a loop was proposed. L–10 trains coming from Fuencarral would run around the loop in alternate directions and then return to the city. This would have created a 58km long line with a very complicated operation scheme. Therefore

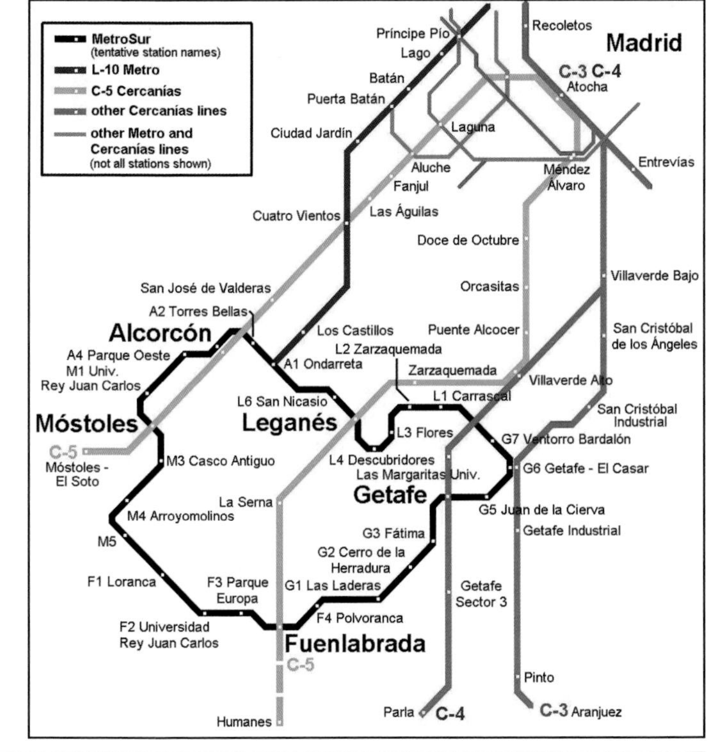

From 2003 MetroSur (future L–12) will connect five important towns south of Madrid. Alcorcón, Móstoles, Fuenlabrada, Getafe and Leganés have a population of approximately one million. the 40km ring line will be totally underground and serve as a feeder for several suburban rail lines.

the final decision was for a separate ring line which connects to L–10 in the town of Alcorcón. Initial plans also proposed an alignment partly above ground, since large areas between the five towns are fields and meadows. However, in order to avoid problems for future developments, a totally underground route was chosen. The whole project, worth €940 million, was divided into six contracts, allowing all major Spanish construction companies to participate. A consortium of ACS and VIAS will build 9.5km of tunnel and five stations between Alcorcón and Móstoles, FCC will bore the 7.3km from Móstoles to Loranca and build five stations. The next 3km will be dug by SACYR and OHL with each firm constructing one station. NECSO will build 6.5km from Fuenlabrada to Pablo Iglesias in southern Getafe with four stations. Ferrovial will undertake the next 7.3km through Getafe to Los Espartales with six stations, and Dragados will do the final 7km through Leganés with five stations. Five large-diameter (9.3m) tunnel boring machines will be used, together with two smaller ones. While the four 1995 tunnel boring machines can be used again, a fifth is required to excavate the harder rock under Getafe. Each of the 27 stations will be 115m long, and an average of 14.5m below ground. In the planning and construction phase, stations are numbered – definitive names will be decided by the corresponding municipalities during the next three years. MetroSur will be operated by new trains (8000-series) ordered from CAF/Alstom/Siemens. The new 3-car trains formed as motor-trailer-motor will allow free movement between carriages, and more cars can be added as passenger numbers rise. The line will be electrified at 1,500Vdc compared to the general 600V on the existing network. A round trip on *MetroSur* will take 58 minutes.

The rest of the metro network will be connected to *MetroSur* by an L–10 extension from a new underground station called Puerta Batán (built between Batán and Campamento) to Alcorcón 1 (Ondarreta) on the *MetroSur* ring line. The new L–10 extension (costing €150million, contracts awarded to Necso-FCC and to Dragados) is 8.2km long in twin tunnels and includes three intermediate stations, one of which (Cuatro Vientos) also allows transfer to the busy *Renfe* C–5 line. Two more stations may be added later between Ciudad Jardín and Cuatro Vientos when the Campamento development is carried out. In order to increase capacities on L–10 and to use large profile rolling stock (2.8m wide and 120m long), some sections of the original suburban line have had to be widened (Batán – Alonso Martínez), necessitating closure from June 2000 until March 2001. Once L–10 continues to Alcorcón, L–5 will serve the remaining stretch between Aluche and Puerta Batán where it will connect to L–10 on the same platform. On the surface section of L–10, an 800m stretch is being covered to improve access to the Casa de Campo Park.

By the end of 2002, L–8 will be extended 5.9km towards Colombia (L–9) and Nuevos Ministerios (transfer to L–6, L–10 and Cercanías). Construction of the extension was awarded to a consortium led by NECSO and began in March 2000. It is partly excavated by a 9.36 diameter tunnelling machine (Mar de Cristal – Colombia) and by the classical *Madrid* method for the section Colombia – Nuevos Ministerios. At the latter station, situated in the business district of Madrid under Paseo de la Castellana, an airport check-in terminal is being built. From Nuevos Ministerios the airport can be reached in 12 minutes. Another station may be added later between Mar de Cristal and Colombia (under Arturo Soria Street), to allow transfer to L–11 which is planned to reach Chamartín. For this extension Madrid applied again for subsidies from EU funds. At the airport end of this line everything is prepared for a future extension towards the new terminals, to be built soon.

L–1 is once again being extended by three stations (3.2km) towards the south to a new housing development. Although the line may be ready in three years, the stations will not open to the public until residents have moved into their new homes. This is the first time an agreement has been reached between regional government and a private building society which will contribute one third of the total cost of this extension. By 2003 the Madrid metro network will be 228km long.

Other works being carried out currently include the covering of a 1.5km section on L–9 through Rivas-Vaciamadrid. A 3km section on the *Renfe Cercanías* route between Atocha and Vallecas is also being put underground through the areas of Entrevías and El Pozo. In southern Madrid, a new 3km avenue will lead from Villaverde-Bajo to Villaverde-Alto, also by covering the existing *Cercanías* tracks. In the north of Madrid's metropolitan area a *Cercanías* extension is almost finished from Cantoblanco via Alcobendas to San Sebastián de los Reyes. In Getafe, the most important station on C–4, Getafe-Centro, is also being put underground and will connect to *MetroSur*. On C–3, a new station called Getafe-El Casar is being built together with *MetroSur*.

Mid-term projects

After 2003, L–11 could become a long line running from the south-west to the east and eventually to CHAMARTÍN in the north. The south-western extension to Carabanchel Alto had already been planned in detail in the mid-1990s but, apart from the short stretch in operation now, it was not included in the definitive expansion programme. West of PAN BENDITO there would be five stations: Torres Garrido, Plaza de la Emperatriz, Joaquín Turina, General Saliquet and LAS ÁGUILAS (C–5). It would make sense to continue towards CUATRO VIENTOS where the *RENFE* C–5 and L–10 will meet soon. Newer plans show L–11 running from PLAZA ELÍPTICA towards ATOCHA-*RENFE* crossing L–3 at PALOS DE LA FRONTERA. East of ATOCHA it would meet L–6 and L–9 at SAINZ DE BARANDA, L–7 at ASCAO and L–5 at CIUDAD LINEAL. From there it would turn north along Arturo Soria Avenue, cross L–4 and L–8 and eventually reach the northern main railway station at CHAMARTÍN.

Another route already considered some ten years ago was the gap between CHAMARTÍN and today's L–4 terminus at PARQUE SANTA MARÍA. Early plans showed a L–10 branch from CHAMARTÍN, but this route could be covered by an extended L–1, which is planned to reach the railway station anyway. So in the future CHAMARTÍN could be served by three metro lines. Also, L–9 might run further north from HERRERA ORIA to Mirasierra by using tracks that link to the metro depot.

The feasibility of a second cross city tunnel via SOL and/or ALONSO MARTÍNEZ is being studied by *RENFE*. The current alignment via RECOLETOS and NUEVOS MINISTERIOS does not really take passengers into the old city centre, most passengers getting off at ATOCHA to take L–1 to SOL or GRAN VÍA. Outside the city of Madrid, the *CERCANÍAS* network will be extended in the south from FUENLABRADA to Humanes, and in the north from TRES CANTOS to Colmenar Viejo. A 14.5km branch will be built off route C3 to Aranjuez towards San Martín de la Vega to provide access to a new Time Warner theme park which is being developed there.

The eastbound tunnel of the MAR DE CRISTAL – CAMPO DE LAS NACIONES section of L–8 was excavated by a Lovat 7.4 diameter TBM which became available after Valencia's metro construction concluded.
Emiliano Durán

BARCELONA METRO

INTRODUCTION

Barcelona, founded by the Romans as Barcino, is the capital of Catalonia (Catalunya), an autonomous part of Spain which consists of the provinces of Girona, Lleida, Tarragona and Barcelona. The city itself has 1.6 million inhabitants and 100 square kilometres and it is Spain's most important Mediterranean harbour and a very popular tourist destination.

The Barcelona urban rail network including extensions planned for 2010 as approved in spring 2000 (subject to changes). Station names given for new lines are for orientation only.

A new logo pole next to an old *art-nouveau* Metro sign marks the entrance to LICEU station on L3 right in the heart of the Rambla, in front of the opera house of the same name. Platforms lie directly under street level with no connection between them, which is unique on the Barcelona metro network.

In the late 1970s, democracy finally became a reality for Spain after almost 40 years of dictatorship under Franco. For Catalonia and Barcelona this meant the recuperation of its own language, Catalan, which now officially coexists with Spanish. Most place names are very similar in Catalan and Spanish, and therefore officially only Catalan names are used. The same is true for station names. This text only uses Catalan place names unless for historic reasons the original Spanish name of a station or company wants to be illustrated. If the reader observes small variations in certain names (for example Cat. Sarrià / Span. Sarriá) it is due to the different spelling in each language.

During the 19th century and as a consequence of industrialisation, the population of Barcelona increased rapidly from 120,000 in 1787 to 250,000 in 1860 and 545,000 in the year 1900. The tearing down of the city walls in 1854 and the city expansion plan by Ildefons Cerdà (Eixample) in 1859 created a new metropolis which at the beginning of the 20th century annexed neighbouring villages like Gràcia, Sant Gervasi, Sarrià, Les Corts, Sants, Sant Andreu and Sant Martí which now form the modern city of Barcelona, one of the most densely populated cities in Europe. To the west Barcelona is limited by the Collserola mountain range, to the east by the Mediterranean Sea, but in the north and in the south the metropolitan area stretches out without any urban disruption towards other big cities like Badalona, Sant Adrià de Besòs and Santa Coloma de Gramanet in the north and L'Hospitalet de Llobregat, Esplugues and Cornellà in the south which are also served by the Barcelona Metro, and which together with the city of Barcelona comprise more than 2.5million inhabitants. The larger metropolitan area served by the *RENFE* suburban service (*RODALIES/CERCANÍAS*) and by the Catalan Railways (*FGC – FERROCARRILS DE LA GENERALITAT DE CATALUNYA*) includes major cities like Sabadell, Terrassa, Sant Cugat, Cerdanyola, Rubí in the Vallès county, Mataró and all the northern coast towns in the Maresme county, and Sant Boi, Gavà, El Prat de Llobregat, Castelldefels and Martorell in the Baix Llobregat county, all of which lie within a radius of 50km of Barcelona and add up to almost 4million inhabitants.

In the year 2000, Barcelona and its metropolitan area are served by two metro services, the city owned *FERROCARRIL METROPOLITÀ DE BARCELONA* (generally referred to as the *METRO* and operating L1, L2, L3, L4 and L5) and the urban service operated by *FGC – FERROCARRILS DE LA GENERALITAT DE CATALUNYA* (owned by the Catalan Government) with its two metro lines U6 and U7 and often still referred to by the people of Barcelona as *TREN DE SARRIÀ*. In this book the history of all metro-type lines will be considered as one, fostering the idea that in the near future the entire network can be used as one (see chapter about 'Tickets and Fare System').

FROM THE BEGINNING TO THE CIVIL WAR

The first metropolitan railway built in Barcelona was the Barcelona – Sarrià Line which opened on 24 June 1863 and ran on the surface from CATALUNYA to SARRIÀ. It is the direct predecessor of today's FGC underground line (now used by U6, S1, S2) to Sarrià and further to Sant Cugat, Terrassa and Sabadell. The alignment followed basically today's line along Balmes Street and then in a curve along Via Augusta to SARRIÀ.

The first horse-drawn tramway was put into service in 1872 between Pla de la Boqueria (near today's LICEU station on the Rambla) and Gràcia, basically the same route of the original metro line (now L3).

At the beginning of the century two metro projects were born in Barcelona, one to connect the harbour to the upper parts of town such as Gràcia and Sant Gervasi, the other to connect existing rail terminals in the south and north of the city.

In 1907, Pau Muller and Gonçal Zaragoza applied for the concession of the first underground railway for Barcelona which should connect the Ciutadella Park and the Estació de França to Bonanova in the upper part of the city. The line would run along Passeig de Colom, Rambla, Plaça Catalunya, Passeig de Gràcia, Gran de Gràcia, Plaça de Lesseps and under Putxet mountain to Passeig de la Bonanova. It would be 7.2km long and have nine stations: Parc, Colom, Sant Josep (at Boqueria market), PLAÇA DE CATALUNYA, Aragó, Jardinets (at the end of Passeig de Gràcia), Josepets (LESSEPS), Avinguda del Tibidabo and Bonanova (at Plaça de la Bonanova). The State approved the project in 1912 but due to lack of finances it could not be realised.

In 1920, one year after the opening of Madrid's metro, interest for the project awoke again. Banco de Vizcaya, to whom the rights for the project had been transferred, reapplied for the concession which was granted in 1921 for 99 years with the condition to finish the project within six years. The newly founded company was called *GRAN METROPOLITANO DE BARCELONA*, S.A. (G.M.B.) and the construction contract was awarded to Hormaeche y Beraza, the company that had built Madrid's first line between SOL and CUATRO CAMINOS. Just after the beginning of construction the initial project was modified, LESSEPS was established as the upper end of the line, because meanwhile tramway service had been improved around the Bonanova area. At the lower end the viability of a line along Passeig de Colom was put in doubt due to its vicinity to the harbour basin. Instead a branch line from ARAGÓN (now PASSEIG DE GRÀCIA) along Via Laietana would be built which could even

Left Inside an original metro car used in the early days of the *METRO TRANSVERSAL* (picture taken 1998). The driver's cabin takes up only a small part of the car's front.

Right This original *METRO TRANVERSAL* carriage was on exhibition at ESTACIÓ DE FRANÇA during 1998 (150 Years of Railways in Spain). The 1672mm gauge allows 3.1m wide carriages.

take advantage of a tunnel that had been excavated by the City in 1908 when this street was cut through the old parts of Barcelona to improve traffic flow. The upper part would be served by all trains, and then from ARAGÓN Line 1 trains would go to CATALUÑA and the Rambla whereas Line 2 trains would go down to URQUINAONA and CORREOS. Construction work finally began in July 1921 and had to be done totally underground along Passeig de Gràcia, where the line had to cross under the *MZA* link line running in a cutting along Aragó Street, and Gran de Gràcia. The section along the Rambla in the old city centre had to be excavated by an open method for its low depth due to underground waters. In March 1923 strikes brought construction to a complete halt for two months, but most of the line could be finished in 1924. The section between Lesseps and Cataluña (now part of L3) was officially inaugurated on 30 December 1924. It was 2.7km long and had two intermediate stations, ARAGÓN and DIAGONAL. Service was provided by ten 2-car trains, and tickets were between 20 and 30 céntimos. Five months later, on 1 May 1925, FONTANA was also opened and on 5 July 1925 the 600m long Rambla section to LICEO was added. From December 1925, the *GRAN METRO* was run by *TRANVÍAS DE BARCELONA*.

While the first line was finished, the *GRAN METRO* had ambitious projects for future expansion, a 5km long and partly surface line from LESSEPS to Sant Gervasi and then to Vallcarca and Horta (similar to today's L3), a circular line from LESSEPS to Sarrià, Les Corts, Sants, Hostafrancs, Poble Sec, Rambla, Catedral and then to Estació de França. From there another line would run along Passeig de Colom to the Rambla.

Construction on the branch line to CORREOS suffered serious delays due to underground waters, especially at the JAIME I site. On 19 December 1926 the section between ARAGÓN (now PASSEIG DE GRÀCIA) and JAIME I (now JAUME I) was put into service. The 1.1km long extension included an intermediate station at URQUINAONA and the two-level turn-off between ARAGÓN and CATALUÑA. Another station named Banco was built between URQUINAONA and JAIME I, next to the cathedral but this was never opened.

From then on, the *GRAN METRO* carried some 20,000 passengers a day, which was below the expected numbers. Fares were lowered and a combined tramway–metro ticket was offered, but this did not help to reduce the deficit. So at the end of 1928 the operation contract with *TRANVÍAS DE BARCELONA* was discontinued. During 1929, when Barcelona hosted the International Exhibition, the *GRAN METRO* carried more than 10million passengers (28,000 a day), but in the following years ridership settled between 20,000 and 25,000 a day. To tackle the resulting financial problems, improvements had to be made to the service, such as better connection to the *Metro Transversal* at Cataluña and the *MZA* station at Aragón. Construction of the extension from Jaime I to Correos would have to begin immediately. For this section the tunnel built in 1908 could be used, but it had to be deepened two metres which once again caused water problems. Eventually this section was inaugurated in the era of the Republic on 20 February 1934, which meant that the Catalan name Correus (Post Office) could also be used for the station. This new section was only 311m long and had only one track, but it was an important service for the lower parts of Barcelona, like the harbour, Ciutadella Park, Estació de França and the Barceloneta neighbourhood. In 1935 passenger numbers rose to 30,000 a day (Correos would later be widened to double track, but it was finally closed in 1972 when L4 was extended to Barceloneta and the Poblenou district).

Meanwhile a second project had been presented in 1910 by Fernando Reyes y Garrido to create an underground link between the numerous railway terminals in the north and the south of the city, and to allow through trains with a central station in the heart of the city. Four different companies were operating around Barcelona at that time, *Caminos de Hierros del Norte de España* served large parts of northern Spain including Madrid and had its Barcelona terminal at Estació del Nord (closed in 1972, now bus station), while *MZA* (*Ferrocarriles de Madrid a Zaragoza y Alicante*) served two lines to France (one along the coast and one inland) and two lines to Tarragona (also one along the coast and one inland). This company had its main terminal at Estació de França which was connected to the southern lines along Aragó street, although originally this company had a station at Plaça Catalunya for its line to Martorell, another at Morrot for its Vilanova line and a third at Av. de Icària near today's Estació de França for its Mataró line. Both companies had Spanish gauge (1672mm) and were integrated in *Renfe* in 1941. Another company was *Ferrocarril Sarrià – Barcelona* (*FSB*) which operated the above mentioned train to Sarrià and was building a tunnel through the Collserola mountain at that time. The company had its surface Barcelona terminal next to Plaça de Catalunya where it still is nowadays, but underground. This line was the first one to be built using European international gauge (1435mm) as it was planned to reach the French border one day (which it never did). Another company called *Camino de Hierro del Nordeste de España* (*NEE*) operated the metre-gauge line from Barcelona-Magòria to Martorell along the right side of the River Llobregat, and later on to Igualada and Manresa. The latter two companies were transferred to the Catalan Autonomous Government in 1979 and their current importance will be described in the chapter: 'Other rail transport in and around Barcelona'. This dispersion of railway stations, which was typical for European cities at that time (and still is in some major European cities like London, Paris, Vienna and Moscow), was reason enough for Fernando Reyes to propose a link railway between the different stations. It should start at Bordeta where there should be a direct link to the *MZA* Tarragona line, then it should continue underground under Sants street and reach Plaça d'Espanya where a new underground terminal for the *NEE* narrow gauge line would be built. Then along Barcelona's main artery Gran Via de les Corts Catalanes up to Plaça Universitat where the line would split into two branches, one along Ronda Universitat, the other along Pelai Street. At Plaça de Catalunya there would be a double station, the lower one close to the Rambla would have a direct access to the Sarrià line. Both branches would meet again at Plaça Urquinaona and continue under Ronda de Sant Pere towards Estació del Nord, where it would connect to the *Norte* lines and behind the station to the *MZA* line to Granollers. A little further to the north-east it would come back to the surface and eventually reach the former Poble Nou station on the Mataró line next to the coast (this station was closed before the huge urban redevelopments preceding the 1992 Olympic Games).

This link line would obviously have to follow the Spanish standard gauge of 1672mm but it would also have electrical traction with 900Vdc and a rigid copper-aluminium overhead line. Influenced by the success of the new metro in Madrid, some Catalan and Basque business men joined Mr. Reyes to found *Ferrocarril Metropolitano de Barcelona, SA* (*FMB*). The project was approved by the Ministry of Public Works in 1922. Concession was granted for 99 years and the line would have to be built within six years. The municipality of Barcelona acquired a large amount of shares of the new company, after some time a third of the capital was the city's property, a fact that gave the company a certain touch of public enterprise. Construction work started officially on 8 June 1922 in the presence of King Alfonso XIII, the patron of Madrid's metro, although works had actually begun some months earlier at the crossroads Gran Via / Urgell. Construction was quite difficult due to heavy traffic along Gran Via, therefore the tunnels had to be excavated underground. The station at PLAÇA D'ESPANYA was then the largest cavern of its kind in the world. The most complicated manoeuvre was the metal bridge built 4.6m on top of the Gran Metro line at PLAÇA CATALUNYA, without interrupting service neither on Barcelona's first metro line nor on the tramway lines running above the construction site on Barcelona's busiest square. Unfortunately there were some accidents during construction, the worst happened on 12 April 1924 when eleven workers died at Gran Via / Villarroel. The high amount of labour made it necessary to bring in workers from other parts of Spain, many of whom stayed in the city after finishing the metro to work for the 1929 Exhibition at Plaça d'Espanya.

While work was progressing on the first *FMB* line (today's L1), the company applied for a concession for no less than seven other lines across Barcelona, among them a line from UNIVERSITAT to ESPANYA via PARAL.LEL where trains would change direction (now served by L2 and L3), an extension of the original line along Gran Via to TETUAN (now also L2), a 5.7km extension to SANT ANDREU along the former main roads of Ribes, Clot and Sagrera (now L1 along Meridiana Ave). Another line would run from Gràcia along Passeig de Sant Joan to ARC DE TRIOMF and then along Pujades street to Sant Martí (now partly L4). A mixed passenger and goods line would branch off the first line and run to Can Tunis where a new free port was being planned (this line has never been built in any form). One more line should have a rather suburban character and provide a 13km link from PLAÇA D'ESPANYA south along Gran Via to El Prat and to the future airport (the first airport single track rail link was eventually built in the 1970s for *RENFE* – a metro airport service has been in discussion for years).

To better distinguish Barcelona's two metro companies the *FMB* was soon to be referred to as *METRO TRANSVERSAL*. The inauguration of the initial section between BORDETA and PLAZA CATALUÑA (now part of L1) took place on 10 June 1926. The latter station was situated at a provisional site under Ronda Universitat while the northbound extension was still under construction. At BORDETA, besides MERCADO NUEVO the only surface station along the line, a depot had been built. The line was 4km long and had nine stations which meant quite a short average distance between them (BORDETA, MERCADO NUEVO, SANS, HOSTAFRANCHS, ESPAÑA, ROCAFORT, URGEL, UNIVERSIDAD and PLAZA CATALUÑA). The *METRO TRANSVERSAL* carried fewer passengers than expected mainly due to the fact that the line was run by the tramway company which obviously did not want to take away passengers from its own lines and therefore kept fares high on the new metro. People of Barcelona still showed a certain reservation when it came to travelling under the streets of their city. In 1928, passenger numbers settled around 15,000 a day which was quite a deficit for the company. As a result, they had to separate from

L1 ESPANYA appeared in green light advertising mobile phones during 1999–2000. On the left the tunnel of the original additional track can be seen. It is now used as a transfer corridor to the *FGC* station which has its terminus further south on the same level. The picture is taken from the footbridge which connects both platforms.

A L1 4000-train is approaching Mercat Nou from the south. The former station Bordeta would be situated in the background. This is one of the two short surface stretches on the metro network, in this case to cross over the Ronda del Mig, a major 6-lane ring road.

the tramway company and lower their fares drastically. As a result and also due to the 1929 International Exhibition passengers almost tripled during the following year. On one day the record of 150,000 passengers was reached. At España a third track was used for special trains running from there to the city centre in order to cope with the increased demand during the Exhibition.

The six year period granted for the construction of the entire line had already expired, so the company had to apply for an extra two years permission to finish the extension from Plaza Cataluña to Estació del Nord, which would have four tracks and allow *Norte* trains to run right into the city centre. The large station on Plaza Cataluña should have been named after the ruling King Alfonso XIII but the arrival of the Spanish republic in 1931 obviously changed these plans. The neighbouring town of L'Hospitalet asked for a metro connection, therefore the original line was extended in the open air from Bordeta to Santa Eulalia. In 1931, a concession for a branch line from Bordeta to the Free Port was granted but the line was never built.

On 1 July 1932 both extensions were inaugurated by the then President of the Catalan Autonomous Government, Francesc Macià. The new station Plaça de Catalunya had four tracks, the outer two being used by the *Metro Transversal* with side platforms, the inner two with a central platform were reserved for *MZA* trains and are now used by the *Renfe* Rodalies and regional trains. This station was totally rebuilt in the late 1980s with a new 100m long ticket hall on top of the four tracks which remained basically the same. Similarly at Triomf–Nord (now Arc de Triomf) a station for both companies was built. Here *Renfe* uses the inner two tracks separated by the outer metro platforms by a supporting wall. In October 1932, a new foot tunnel at Plaça de Catalunya provided a better connection between the two metro lines.

The southern extension to Bordeta-Cotxeres (Bordeta-Depot later renamed Santa Eulalia) was only 400m away from Bordeta and initially had only one track. These two extensions produced a heavy increase in passenger numbers and even led to capacity problems during peak hours. In 1933, 54,000 people were carried daily and a flat fare was introduced for the entire line. Due to this success the line was immediately extended further north-east to Marina where a new station, which in the beginning only had one platform, was opened on 1 April 1933. This was the first *Metro Transversal* station to be equipped with an escalator. In April 1935 at Santa Eulalia a bridge was built across the *MZA* rail tracks which greatly improved access to that station, making it the busiest on the whole line. By the end of that year the *Metro Transversal* carried 65,000 passengers a day.

Meanwhile projects for further extension on both ends to Sagrera and Zona Franca were studied. But none of these projects was realised during the following years, although the extension to Sagrera was eventually built in the 1950s.

The Barcelona – Sarrià Line (now U6) started operating between Plaça de Catalunya and Sarrià as a suburban steam railway as soon as 1863, the same year the London *Metropolitan Railway* began running along the first urban underground route, also using steam traction. The Sarrià line had then only five stations (Plaza de Cataluña, Gracia 1, Gracia 2, San Gervasio, Sarriá) and 1672mm gauge. A stop at Provenza was established in 1882 and another one followed in 1887 at Bonanova. On leaving Plaça de Catalunya the line had to cross the former *MZA* line to Martorell on an elevated structure, which was dismantled in 1883 after this company built its link line in a cutting along Aragó street (now covered). The Sarrià Line ran on Balmes street and further up, partly in a cutting around San Gervasio with a short tunnel near today's Muntaner station. At the end of the century, the Sarrià Line already carried some 2million passengers a year.

In 1904/1905 the line was electrified (the first electric rail line in Spain) and changed to international gauge (1435mm). In 1906 the company built a branch line to the newly built Vallvidrera Funicular Railway. The Sarrià Line caused a lot of people to move to the upper parts of Barcelona, therefore a new stop was built along the line at Muntaner in 1908.

From 1916 on, a new company called *Ferrocarriles de Cataluña* extended the line through the Collserola mountain to Les Planes and later to Sant Cugat, Terrassa and Sabadell. Along Balmes street the line was protected by wooden fences, which was like a wall straight through the Eixample district. With the suburban expansion of the line, traffic increased on this urban stretch and although there was a level crossing at all transversal Eixample streets, road traffic was disrupted to such an extent that the city protested against it. The solution was to put the rail line underground. Construction began in 1926 and the section between Plaça de Catalunya and Muntaner was inaugurated on 24 April 1929, just in time for the International Exhibition. From this day on the Sarrià Line can be considered a real metro line, offering a mixed urban and suburban service (similar to the service operated by Japanese subway networks) between Plaça de Catalunya and Sarrià (4.6km). During the construction period a provisional station was erected between Gran Via and Ronda Universitat. In Gràcia construction included the turn-off of the future branch to Avinguda Tibidabo, and therefore the original line was provisionally relocated following Balmes street also in its upper section. Train operation was maintained during the whole three year period of construction.

In July 1936, when the Spanish Civil War broke out, operation of the *Gran Metro* and the *Metro Transversal* was taken over by the workers' committees for the next three years. As in Madrid, metro stations and tunnels served as a refuge for the people during air raids, which the metro survived with only small damage to some coaches. During the war, the *Metro Transversal* was fulfilling its function as a link railway in order to carry ammunition between the different rail terminals. For this purpose a tunnel was built under Pelai Street to provide a link to the Sarrià Line.

The only preserved station pavilion can be seen at Sant Gervasi on the U6 Sarrià Line. Elevators take passengers down to the platforms, which lie in a curve and thus a London style 'Mind the gap' message can be heard. Entrance to Pl. Molina on the U7 Tibidabo branch is just to the left.

FROM THE POST-WAR PERIOD TO THE AMALGAMATION OF THE TWO METROS

After the Spanish Civil War the different metro lines were the least damaged means of transport in the city, so they had to cope with most of the demand, which made it necessary to order new coaches and to double tracks along the JAIME I – CORREOS section. For Spain a 36-year long period of dictatorship under General Franco began which meant that Spanish was once again the only language to be used in public life, and that all metro stations had to carry exclusively Spanish names instead of Catalan used during the republican period. On 15 April 1946 a new *GRAN METRO* station was opened at FERNANDO on the Rambla which used a 145m long tunnel, previously built for train reversing beyond LICEO and which was only single track with one platform. In those days *GRAN METRO* proposed three more projects, which were not realised. The CORREOS branch would be extended to the França railway station, the upper part of the line would be extended from LESSEPS to Pàdua Street and an intermediate station would be built at Travessera de Gràcia, between FONTANA and DIAGONAL. Although no extensions were built for the Gran Metro, passenger numbers settled around 35million a year on this line.

At the same time, the *METRO TRANSVERSAL* had to fight against nationalisation. After the civil war most mainline rail companies were in serious trouble, and all of the Spanish gauge lines were integrated into *RENFE* (*RED NACIONAL DE LOS FERROCARRILES ESPAÑOLES*) in January 1941. As the *METRO TRANSVERSAL* was planned as a link railway it also used 1672mm Spanish gauge and therefore was included in the nationalisation process. For two years the exclusively urban service on this line was under the direction of *RENFE*, but finally the city succeeded in convincing the Spanish authorities of the line's municipal character. In 1943 it was handed back to the semi-municipal company.

New trains of the 200-series were ordered and put into service during the next years. The extension plans towards Sant Andreu were reactivated, although the alignment had to be changed according to the new Raillink Plan, which included a mainline tunnel together with the metro along the new Meridiana artery. GLORIAS station was designed to allow a future branch along Gran Via (which was never built). The first stretch of this new extension was inaugurated on 23 June 1951 (MARINA – CLOT: 1.8km), the first new section of this line for 17 years. Ridership grew rapidly after that to some 165,000 passengers a day, which on certain days during the celebration of the 'Eucharistic Congress' reached more than 320,000. This tendency was very encouraging for the construction progress of the extension to Sant Andreu. On 8 May 1953 a 600m section from CLOT to NAVAS was put into service. Some months later, on 26 January 1954 the line reached SAGRERA (690m) and on 15 May 1954 FABRA Y PUIG (850m). The line was then 11km long and carried 243,000 passen-

L1 GLÒRIES – a typical 3-platform station on the Sant Andreu extension of the line built in the 1950s. Originally meant to separate passenger flows, today doors open on both sides at the same time and people get on and off on either side. The orange signs next to the stairs indicate that this exit is not open at the moment.

Until a new panelling scheme was introduced in the 1980s, Barcelona's metro logo and station name panels were similar to those in Madrid and those still in use on *FGC* lines.

gers a day during 1955. From 1953 new trains of the 300-series were introduced which allowed a more frequent service. For a future extension of the line two variants were discussed: turning right after Fabra y Puig straight into the heart of the town of Sant Andreu, or further on along Meridiana Avenue. Eventually the first option was chosen, although the line would not reach Torras y Bages until 1968.

During the 1950s Barcelona, like all other major Spanish cities, experienced heavy immigration from all parts of Spain. Large residential areas were built all around Barcelona and new needs for public transport arose. The city government began to study the possibility of building a *Transversal Alto* (Upper transversal line) from Congreso and Sagrera to Gràcia and Sants (which later became the L5 route). As no money was available the decision was taken to construct only two short branch lines, one from Sagrera to Horta, and another one from Sans (now Plaça de Sants) to San Ramón (now Collblanc). The latter one was initially meant to use Spanish gauge like the *Metro Transversal* line, but this plan was changed soon to allow its future connection to what became L5. This section would not be finished until 1969. The northern branch to Horta was originally planned to start at Navas and also to use Spanish gauge, but finally in 1955 construction of the Sagrera – Vilapiscina section (2.2km) started with the intention of creating a totally new line with international gauge. For this line trains of the 600-series were ordered and inauguration took place on 21 July 1959. The first new line (then called Línea 2) since the 1920s had five stations, Sagrera, Viviendas del Congreso, Maragall, Virrey Amat and Vilapiscina. In 1960 this line was the first line in the world to be equipped with an automatic train operation system, a predecessor of today's ATO standard.

In 1952 the City Council had taken the decision to municipalize all transport companies (except the Sarrià Line) operating in the city of Barcelona. This was actually the beginning of Barcelona's current metro network. In June 1956 a new transfer tunnel was built at Cataluña which provided a uniform network at least between these two metro companies. A unified tariff system was established and soon more than 70,000 people a day used the transfer corridor at Cataluña. In February 1960 both metro companies (*Gran Metro* and *Metro Transversal*) were finally merged into *Ferrocarril Metropolitano de Barcelona* (*FCMB*).

U6 U7 Gràcia – a 111-series train heading for Universitat Autònoma in this 4-track junction which was refurbished in the late 1990s. The outer tracks behind the pillars are used by U7 to Av. Tibidabo.

In 1940 the city had resumed construction of the missing underground sections of the Sarrià Line, namely from MUNTANER to TRES TORRES. The new underground stations of BONANOVA and TRES TORRES opened for traffic on 12 May 1952, although they were not officially inaugurated until 20 June 1953. Plans were designed to connect the Sarrià Line to the *GRAN METRO*. The first plan proposed a tunnel between DIAGONAL and GRACIA, so that the Sarrià Line section between GRACIA and PLAZA DE CATALUÑA could be used exclusively by the *FERROCARRILES DE CATALUÑA* suburban services. The second plan was for a short connecting tunnel from PLAZA DE CATALUÑA to URQUINAONA, and to link it to the CORREOS branch of the *GRAN METRO*. None of these plans was realised and service on the Avinguda del Tibidabo line (now U7) started on 1 January 1954, operating as a branch of the Sarrià Line with four stations, PLAZA MOLINA, PADUA, NÚÑEZ DE ARCE (now PUTXET) and AVENIDA TIBIDABO (now AVINGUDA TIBIDABO). The last station lies very deep and was therefore equipped with an elevator. Further plans for this branch included a 780m extension to the bottom station of the Tibidabo Funicular, but due to the steep slope of the mountain this would have meant at least a 68m deep station reached by lifts. Service between the two lines is still provided today by the historic *TRAMVIA BLAU*. Meanwhile construction was restarted at the line's PLAZA DE CATALUÑA terminal, where parallel platforms were built to separate urban and suburban services (finished in 1959). The total length of the urban sections of the Sarrià line was then 6.4km (4.6km PLAZA DE CATALUÑA – SARRIÁ, 1.8km GRACIA – AVINGUDA TIBIDABO) and it had 11 underground stations and one on the surface (SARRIÁ).

THE 1960s AND 1970s

After the former two metro companies (*GRAN METRO* and *METRO TRANSVERSAL*) had been merged into one municipal company, numbers for the existing lines were introduced. Thus the original *METRO TRANSVERSAL* line between SANTA EULALIA and FABRA Y PUIG became *Línea* I, the newest line from SAGRERA to VILAPISCINA became *Línea* II (now part of L5) and actually Barcelona's first metro line from LESSEPS to CORREOS and FERNANDO was from now on *Línea* III. Both lines were in bad need of modernisation, and therefore in the early 1960s new trains were bought for L1 (400-series) and L3 (300C-series). At LESSEPS and FONTANA the old elevators were substituted by modern escalators, and L1's three surface stations, MERCADO NUEVO, BORDETA and SANTA EULALIA were refurbished with 90m long platforms to allow service with 4- or 5-car trains.

In 1960, Barcelona's population had grown to 1.5million, which showed an obvious need for more high capacity transport lines. In 1963 an Urgent Plan was approved, which included three important parts: 1– extension of existing lines, 2– four new lines and 3– suburban lines.

Left L5 SAGRADA FAMÍLIA – a repainted 1000-series train heading for HORTA. From here the line should have continued straight ahead to Badalona but was provisionally connected to what was planned as Line 2, for which a station was completely built just around the corner on almost the same level.

Facing page L4 PASSEIG DE GRÀCIA – a 1000-series train arriving from URQUINAONA. This connecting tunnel was opened in 1995 for transfer to L2 which unfortunately cannot be reached by a lift from here. On the floor you can observe the guide rails for the blind.

A total of 13km would be added to the three existing lines: L1 from FABRA Y PUIG to TORRAS Y BAGES, and from SANS (now PLAÇA DE SANTS) to SAN RAMÓN (now COLLBLANC); L2 (now L5) from VILAPISCINA to HORTA and from SAGRERA to SANS; L3 from FERNANDO to ESPAÑA and from LESSEPS to Vallirana Street, plus the tunnel mentioned before to connect this line to the Sarrià Line at PLAÇA DE CATALUNYA.

At the next stage four new lines would be built: the fourth line would run from MARAGALL to PLAZA DE CATALUÑA (basically today's L4), then to SANT ANTONI and along Urgell Street to Pl. Calvo Sotelo (now Francesc Macià) (not served by any line until today) and along Trav. de les Corts to ZONA UNIVERSITARIA (similar to today's L3) and then to SAN RAMÓN (now COLLBLANC). The fifth line was designed to be semi-circular, similar to today's planned L9, from ALFONSO X via SAN GERVASIO and Calvo Sotelo (Francesc Macià) to PL. ESPAÑA. The sixth line would start at França station and follow Passeig de Sant Joan to TETUAN, then turn right and run along Gran Via to Badalona (not realised at all). The seventh line would start at MARINA and serve Poblenou (like today's L4 as far as LA PAU) and continue to Santa Coloma (not yet built).

The first stage of this ambitious plan should have been carried out between 1964 and 1967, but it suffered some delays. In 1965, another short extension was added to the plan: the Sarrià Line should get another station in the heart of the former independent town of Sarrià, called DUQUE DE GANDÍA (now REINA ELISENDA). Construction work on all extensions started during 1964–65. Meanwhile passenger numbers on the three metro lines had grown rapidly during the early 1960s to 210million in 1965 (577,000 a day). Therefore new rolling stock (300C- and 400-series) had to be ordered to be ready for service when the first extension would be operative.

Like Spain's capital Madrid, Barcelona kept growing and new residential areas appeared wherever they could. Also like Madrid, plans for metro expansion kept changing during the 1960s. In 1966, a second urgent plan was published which included 48km of new lines, thus reaching a total network of 86km (plus the Sarrià Line) within 11 years. This plan was interesting as it incorporated certain social principles. The metro should be a public service and not a business; it should serve all populated areas; the network should not be concentrated in the city centre, and transfer should be avoided where possible. Distance between stations was planned to be some 700m on average. The 1966 plan differed to the 1963 Urgent Plan, by saying that Line II should run from HORTA via SAGRADA FAMILIA to the city centre (UNIVERSIDAD), and to PUEBLO SECO (now PARAL.LEL) (10km, like today's central part of L2). Line III would become a ring line around the left side of the Eixample district, similar to its current alignment but connecting ZONA UNIVERSITARIA to LESSEPS via SARRIÁ (12.8km). Line IV would also be a circular line on the right side of the Eixample, the same as it is today but with a link between MARAGALL and VERNEDA via Sant Andreu (16.5km). Line V would run parallel to the sea between SAN RAMÓN (now COLLBLANC) and VERNEDA (11km, like today's L5 and L2). Line VI would follow Diagonal Avenue for most of its length, i.e. from ZONA UNIVERSITARIA to GLORIAS and then along Gran Via to Barrio del Besós (now BESÒS) (10.5km, this route may be served by the new tram in the future), and Line VII would run from SANT ANTONI along Urgell up to Plaça Bonanova (5km, not built at all).

Construction work for the first section of this important plan started in December 1968 between SAGRADA FAMILIA and PUEBLO SECO (now PARAL.LEL). Other parts followed in 1969: PUEBLO SECO – MARIA CRISTINA – ZONA UNIVERSITARIA (Lines III and VI), GRAN VÍA (now PG. DE GRÀCIA) – JOANICH (IV), SAN RAMÓN – PUBILLA CASAS (V) and CORREOS – SELVA DE MAR (IV). Whereas most sections opened after some years, Line II between SAGRADA FAMÍLIA and PARAL.LEL took 27 years to be put into service.

While preparation began for these new lines, construction of the extensions included in the

1963 urgent plan were finished and new sections were successively opened to the public. The first was the 690m stretch from Vilapiscina to Horta on *Línea* II which opened on 5 October 1967.

On 14 March 1968, L1 reached Torras y Bages, a 1,900m long section that crossed the old part of Sant Andreu diagonally, the first line not running directly under streets. There is another station in the heart of the neighbourhood, then called San Andrés.

On L3, the provisional station at Fernando was closed on 1 March 1968 and the line was extended 630m to Atarazanas (now Drassanes) on 14 December 1968. In 1969 platforms were lengthened at Diagonal and Cataluña, where also a new access (today's rotunda) was built.

A year later, on 3 November 1969, the first part of the new transversal line L5 between San Ramón (now Collblanc) and Diagonal-Rambla Cataluña was inaugurated. It was 4.3km long and had seven new stations (San Ramón, Badal, Sans, Roma, Entenza, Hospital, Diagonal-Rambla Cataluña).

L3 reached its new terminus at Pueblo Seco (now Paral.lel) on 17 June 1970 (627m). From here a funicular railway climbs up the Montjuïc mountain.

Only a few days later, on 26 June, the second part of L5 between Diagonal and Sagrera (4km) was also put into service. It included four new stations, General Mola (now Verdaguer), Sagrada Familia, Dos de Mayo (now Hospital Sant Pau) and Campo del Arpa. The northern part between Sagrada Familia and Sagrera was connected to *Línea* V only provisionally, as it was planned to be part of *Línea* II in the future. Therefore a second station, named Gaudí, was built next to Sagrada Familia under Gaudí Avenue. In the early 1990s, when construction of L2 was resumed, this totally built station was not included and a new one was constructed for L2. Platforms of this ghost station can be seen from L5 trains pulling out of Sagrada Família station towards Horta.

The Barcelona metro network had grown to 30km by 1970 (plus 6.4km Sarrià Line). Metro maps showed lines in different colours, *Línea* I was black, *Línea* II: blue, *Línea* III: green, *Línea* V: purple and the future *Línea* IV: red. The short stretch under construction of *Línea* VI (later L3 along Diagonal Ave.) was shown in brown. Later in the mid-1970s today's line colours were introduced. Due to an increase in car traffic in those years the new extensions did not help much to increase passenger numbers, which settled around 200million a year. Between 1970 and 1973 new trains of the 1000-series began operating (these trains were still running in the year 2000 on L4 and L5).

So far the Barcelona metro only served the city of Barcelona, although Santa Eulalia was located in the neighbouring town of L'Hospitalet. The strong immigration during the previous decades created densely populated towns all around Barcelona, especially Cornellà, Santa Coloma de Gramanet and Badalona, the latter two being separated from Barcelona by the river Besòs. So while new extensions totalling some 25km were under construction, an updated metro plan was designed and published in 1971, the same year the last tramway disappeared from Barcelona's streets. This was a very ambitious plan that aimed to reach a 112km network with 141 stations (in the year 2000, Barcelona's metro has 80km plus the Sarrià Line). Some of the proposals made then re-appear in the current 2001–2010 plan. L1 would reach Residencia Sanitaria (now Feixa Llarga) in the south, and

U6 Sarrià – a 111-series train is arriving from Reina Elisenda on a U6 service to Pl. Catalunya. One of *FGC's* workshops is located to the left, in the open.

the northern slope of the Collserola Mountain where the 1982 Universal Exhibition was planned to be held. L2 (now L5) would reach Teixonera (hopefully to be built soon). L3 would not be a ring line, but continue to Vall d'Hebron in the north and to Esplugues in the southwest (only construction of the northern extension was carried out). L4 would not become a ring line either, but run to Guineueta (now Via Júlia) and to Bon Pastor (now part of the L9 project). L5 would run to San Ildefonso, and to Badalona (now L4). A new Line 6 would run all the way from Zona Franca to Sant Adrià and Santa Coloma similar to today's L9 project.

On 20 March 1972 Correos station was closed again. On 4 April Jaime I and Urquinaona also had to be shut in order to incorporate this part of the former *Gran Metro* into the new *Línea* IV. Under the crossroads of Passeig de Gràcia and Gran Via a new station was built, then called Gran Vía (now Passeig de Gràcia). After this station the newly built section had to be connected to the original line near the *Gran Metro* Aragón junction. This meant very tight curves (easily audible today) which L4 trains have to pass at a very low speed. The original junction still exists as a connecting tunnel between L3 and L4. The new L4 started operation on 5 February 1973 between Jaime I and Plaza Joanich (3.5km, of which 2.5km were newly built) with four intermediate stations (Urquinaona, Gran Vía, Gerona and General Mola). On 22 December 1973 the long transfer tunnel between today's L3 and L4 Passeig de Gràcia stations opened. The same day L4 started running, L5 was extended 1km from San Ramón to Pubilla Casas which lies in L'Hospitalet.

Before inaugurations continued during the next years, an updated metro plan was issued in 1974. But there was little variation from the 1971 plan. Instead of L1, L3 should run to Ciutat Meridiana in the north of Barcelona. Instead of Line 6, L4 should continue to Santa Coloma, a town that should also be reached by L1 from Torras y Bages. This plan also included a L5 extension into the centre of Cornellà. This was the first plan that considered concepts like environmental improvements, energy savings or integration of all public transport.

The first inauguration to take place in the following four years was the L4 extension to Guinardó (1.5km) on 16 May 1974, with an intermediate station at Alfonso X.

While the metro was celebrating its 50th birthday, L3 began operating on an isolated stretch between Roma-Estación Renfe (now Sants-Estació) and Zona Universitaria on 20 January 1975: 3.1km with four intermediate stations, Plaza Centro, Les Corts, María Cristina and Palacio. The original part between María Cristina and Zona Universitaria, supposed to form a future Line 6, was definitely included into L3. Six months later the missing section between Pueblo Seco (now Paral.lel) and Roma was inaugurated on 15 July 1975 by the still Princes of Spain, Juan Carlos and Sofía. This section is 2.6km long and includes three intermediate stations, Parlamento (now Poble Sec), España and Tarragona. The two new sections of L3 were equipped with third rail power supply whereas the older part used an overhead wire. Therefore for the following seven years passengers had to change trains at Pueblo Seco and the new section was called *IIIB*. That same day, the *Renfe* single track airport line opened for traffic.

On 15 March 1976, L4 reached Barceloneta (760m), a station that also served the *Renfe* terminus of the former Mataró suburban line, which was located near Estació de França and which was abandoned and demolished in the early 1990s when all suburban lines started operating as cross-city lines.

On 2 October 1976, also the Sarrià Line extension from Sarriá to Duque de Gandía (now Reina Elisenda) was put into service. This station lies closer to the centre of Sarrià than the eponymous station which was also rebuilt and covered. Now it has four tracks, of which the western two are used for trains going to Reina Elisenda which have to cross the main tracks before arriving at Sarrià station. In the 1970s the company operating this line, together with the suburban lines to Sant Cugat, Terrassa and Sabadell got into serious financial trouble, so in 1977 the network was transfered to *FEVE* (Spanish narrow gauge railways) before it was handed over to the new Catalan administration in 1978. One year later a new public company called *Ferrocarrils de la Generalitat de Catalunya* was founded which still operates the Sarrià Line today.

L5 kept growing into the town of Cornellà, and trains started running to San Ildefonso on 23 November 1976. The new 2.3km section included two intermediate stations, Maladeta (now Can Vidalet) and Buxeres (now Can Boixeres) which is on the surface, though covered, and where a depot was built for the new cars of the 1000-series.

Despite many constructional problems due to water infiltration, L4 opened parallel to the coast line on 7 October 1977 between BARCELONETA and SELVA DE MAR to serve the neighbourhood of Poblenou. This 4km long section included four intermediate stations, RIBERA (now CIUTADELLA-VILA OLÍMPICA), PERE IV (planned as Alava, now BOGATELL), LUCHANA (now LLACUNA) and POBLE NOU (planned as Bilbao).

After this last expansion in the 1970s the total network had reached 48.8km and passenger numbers had climbed to 266million a year which meant a 25 per cent increase. During that period *RENFE* built a new connecting tunnel between PLAÇA DE CATALUNYA and SANTS stations. Therefore UNIVERSITAT metro station on L1 had to be totally rebuilt to allow *RENFE* trains to cross under the southbound metro track. Platforms for the new metro station were built on two different levels, lying almost on top of each other.

During 1975, Spain's dictator Franco died and slowly democracy returned to Spain. For a couple of years Spanish names remained on metro maps, but some new stations were named in Catalan straight from the beginning, like POBLE NOU (instead of Spanish Pueblo Nuevo). Catalunya regained its autonomous government which, from 1981, was responsible for the financing and planning of infrastructure in the city and its metropolitan area. This transfer brought investment and construction to a temporary halt, and it took several years until new extensions could be opened to the public.

BARCELONA METRO – THE LAST 20 YEARS

After the Catalan Government (*Generalitat*) was re-established in 1979, the Sarrià Line together with the suburban lines to Sabadell and Terrassa and the narrow gauge lines from PLAÇA ESPANYA to Manresa and Igualada were handed over to the newly founded company *FERROCARRILS DE LA GENERALITAT DE CATALUNYA* (*FGC*). The four existing metro lines remained the property of the City of Barcelona, but from now on the Generalitat was in charge of planning and financing any new lines. In the early 1980s, construction on various extensions, which had been stopped by the Spanish state was slowly resumed.

On 19 April 1982 the president of the Catalan government, Jordi Pujol, inaugurated a 3.4km extension on L4 from GUINARDÓ to ROQUETES (now VIA JÚLIA) with two stations in between, MARAGALL and LLUCMAJOR. Between these last two stations there is a distance of 1,670m, as the line runs very close to L5 between MARAGALL and VIRREI AMAT. A few months later L4 expanded at the other end from SELVA DE MAR to LA PAU (15 October 1982), which included 2.6km and two intermediate stations, MINA (now BESÒS MAR) and BESÒS.

MERCAT NOU on L1 is Barcelona's only surface station. The tunnel portal towards PLAÇA DE SANTS can be seen in the background. Just to the left, *RENFE* lines enter the cross-city tunnel from the south.

L1 SANTA EULÀLIA – a 4000-series train heading for FEIXA LLARGA is entering the tunnel after the short surface stretch parallel to the *RENFE* alignment. This station was rebuilt and covered when the line was extended under the *RENFE* tracks to TORRASSA in 1983. In the future a new interchange station will be built between these two stations.

On 21 December 1983 the metro finally crossed the River Besòs in a tunnel to reach SANTA COLOMA. The 2km long L1 section has two intermediate stations at TRINITAT VELLA and BARÓ DE VIVER. Two days later, on 23 December, L1 was extended at the other end from SANTA EULÀLIA to TORRASSA. On 5 July 1980 the BORDETA – SANTA EULÀLIA section was closed to build a new covered station at SANTA EULÀLIA. On the day L1 was extended to TORRASSA, BORDETA station was permenantly closed, although platforms are still visible on this short surface stretch of L1. It is still used by drivers for access to the adjacent original depot. From then on, MERCAT NOU is the only open surface station on the Barcelona metro network.

That same day, on 23 December 1983, the first L5 train arrived at CORNELLÀ station, which is situated in the centre of the town and under the existing *RENFE* station. The new section is 1.5km long and has one intermediate station called GAVARRA.

On 22 April 1985 the metro crossed the River Besòs for the second time to arrive at Badalona. Initially this section was planned to be part of *Línea* V from SAGRADA FAMÍLIA to Badalona, but it was now provisionally added to L4. The current expansion plan still shows this stretch as part of L2 which uses a rigid overhead wire whereas L4 was equipped with a third rail. The new section is almost 4km long and has five stations, VERNEDA, JOAN XXIII, SANT ROC, GORG and PEP VENTURA.

For a long time JOAN XXIII carried the annex 'provisional'. The station was supposed to be called Sant Adrià, a small municipality between Barcelona and Badalona. However, the station exits are actually on Badalona municipal territory, so neighbours approaching the station from this side rejected their station being called after the nearby town. The PEP VENTURA terminus is some 700m from the centre of Badalona, therefore this city has always been asking for a further extension which is now included in the 2001–2010 plan.

During the first years of the 1980s the metro changed its image drastically. A new panelling scheme was introduced, some stations were renamed or Catalanised, and train operation was improved to modern standards. All lines have since been supervised from a central control room; they were refitted with ATP (automatic train protection); new ticket vending machines were installed and new trains were ordered for L1 and L3 along with additional trailers for L4 and L5. In 1984 the Catalan government approved its first expansion plan, which compared to the previous ones from the 1970s was not ambitious at all. It basically included extending L1 from SANTA COLOMA to FONDO and from TORRASSA to FEIXA LLARGA, and L2 from UNIVERSITAT to LA PAU. The *FGC* Line terminating at ESPANYA would continue towards the city centre to UNIVERSITAT, using the tunnel excavated for L2 between SANT ANTONI and UNIVERSITAT.

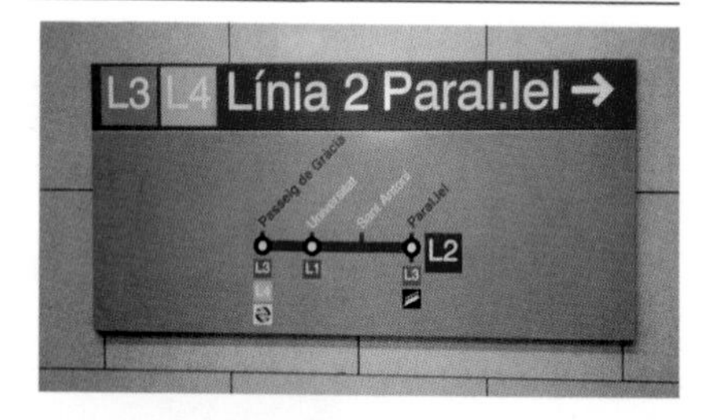

Meanwhile construction on L3 from LESSEPS to MONTBAU had progressed and opened for traffic on 6 November 1985. This 3.1km long extension includes four new stations, VALLCARCA, PENITENTS, VALL D'HEBRON and MONTBAU. PENITENTS is the deepest station, at 23m, on the Barcelona metro network.

Finally on 24 April 1987 the metro reached the centre of L'Hospitalet, Catalunya's second largest city. L1 was extended from TORRASSA to AV. CARRILET. This 2.3km long section includes three intermediate stations, FLORIDA, CAN SERRA and RAMBLA JUST OLIVERAS (transfer to *RENFE*). At AVINGUDA CARRILET a transfer station was built to the *FGC* line along the Llobregat river.

Two years later, on 19 October 1989, a further 2km extension to FEIXA LLARGA (huge hospital complex) was inaugurated. There is only one intermediate station in the middle of the large dormitory town of BELLVITGE. On 18 February 1992, L1 reached its full length arriving at FONDO (780m). This station meant a new beginning for metro station planning in Barcelona as it is the first fully accessible station of the network. Elevators from the street to the ticket hall and down to the platforms were installed and for the blind the access is marked on the floor.

Meanwhile not much work had been done to resume construction on L2. When Barcelona was chosen to host the 1992 Olympic Games the project was rediscovered with the idea to extend the line to the mountain of Montjuïc where the Olympic Stadium and Pavilion were built at that time. No political decision was taken in time and eventually, in 1991, it was too late to build a full metro line to serve during the Olympics. The tunnels and stations excavated almost 20 years earlier between SANT ANTONI and SAGRADA FAMÍLIA had to be rebuilt to adapt them to modern standards of accessibility. Scheduled to open in 1992, this first stretch opened three years later on 25 September 1995.

The new line was given the colour purple and was 3.7km long with six stations, SANT ANTONI, UNIVERSITAT, PASSEIG DE GRÀCIA, TETUAN, MONUMENTAL and SAGRADA FAMÍLIA. All stations were equipped with lifts from the street to the platform level. At UNIVERSITAT a huge 2-level entrance hall was built (as L1 platforms lie on two different levels), but unfortunately not the best solution was chosen for the arrangement of escalators. Level 2 can only be reached by stairs and the lift, and transferring

Top Orientation is made easy by clear and simple panels. At any time trains run from one end to the other on all lines.

Left L2 PASSEIG DE GRÀCIA – a large vestibule was built under Gran Via, one of Barcelona's main thoroughfares. All stations on L2 are easily accessible by lifts and escalators, but access to L4 and L3 is only via L2 platforms and stairs.

passengers have to walk an unnecessary distance. At Passeig de Gràcia transfer to L4 is relatively easy, though not perfect. L2 platforms are accessible by lifts and escalators, but transfer to L4 is only possible by climbing stairs. Transfer to L3 can only be done via L4. At Sagrada Família a totally new station had to be built, although previously a station had been constructed under Gaudí Avenue. However, the new alignment towards Clot did not allow the use of this station. Here, transfer to L5 is quite a long walk, two levels up and then one level down again. All stations were equipped with electronic information panels which show the time remaining for the next train to arrive and other messages of interest to passengers, such as disruptions on any metro line.

After the authorities had realised that football fans, concert goers and tourists also reach the stadium and Palau Sant Jordi on foot, by bus, by open-air escalators or by funicular, the idea of extending L2 up the mountain was abandoned. Instead, the previously built tunnel to Paral.lel was adapted and since 6 January 1996 L2 terminates there. Paral.lel is the most user-friendly transfer station on the Barcelona network, with cross-platform transfer between L2 and L3 (direction Zona Universitària). L2 trains coming from Sant Antoni change tracks before entering the station to provide this easy transfer. The second platform is only used when trains are taken out of service. Unfortunately, operation on both lines is not co-ordinated, and too often a train on one line just leaves while the other is pulling into the station.

This original section of L2 has the curious feature that trains operate on the left between Paral.lel and Monumental. For the first time in Barcelona, the tunnel was built using a tunnel boring machine. In the curve between Tetuan and Monumental both single track tunnels cross each other to continue on the opposite side. After Monumental both tunnels merge before arriving at Sagrada Família. At Passeig de Gràcia, Tetuan and Monumental stations are also in a single track tube, which is only connected to the other at the end of the platform (at Pg. de Gràcia also in the middle where the stairs towards L4 Pep Ventura are situated). Universitat station lies in a double track tunnel, although platforms are separated by a supporting wall. This line uses a rigid overhead wire for current collection. Trains of the new 2000-series had been delivered by CAF some years before opening and ran on L3, for some time. They are equipped with ATO/ATP and air-conditioning. From the outside they look very much like the 3000-series running on L3 but these are the first of the walk-through type, i.e. carriages are connected by an articulated element which helps to better distribute passengers and give them a higher feeling of security. For the first two years, until the line was extended to La Pau, only 3-car trains were used. Station panels are somewhat different from the

L2 Sant Antoni – one of the few central platform stations on the network. On this section trains run on the left. This train leaving for Paral.lel might run from this station to the Fairgrounds via Poble Sec, one day in the future.

scheme introduced on the other lines during the 1980s. Instead of a broad ribbon in the line's colour carrying the station name and the metro symbol, and a narrow grey ribbon on top of it showing all pictograms and exit and transfer directions, L2 used an inverted scheme. The station name appears in white on a grey background, while pictograms have a purple background. At the time of opening L2, a new metro logo was also created. The traditional blue M on white background within a red diamond-shaped frame was substituted by a white M on a red diamond. Station entrances got a new round illuminated M symbol on a pole, which is far more visible than the traditional flat square logo.

Left L2 Bac de Roda – the roof is flat at the ends and vaulted in the middle. Stylish but uncomfortable benches take up a considerable part of the platforms. The indicator shows the remaining time for the next train to arrive.

Below L2 Sant Martí – this station can be distinguished by its dark blue ceiling and the wedge style lamps.

After the long delays suffered during the previous decades, people in the district of Sant Martí feared that this might happen again on the remaining section of L2 and put strong pressure on the government to finish the SAGRADA FAMÍLIA – LA PAU section as soon as possible. Two years later, and again in time for Barcelona's city festival 'Mercè', the new section started operating on 20 September 1997. The new 3.9km section has four intermediate stations, ENCANTS, CLOT, BAC DE RODA and SANT MARTÍ. This section was originally planned to be part of *Línea* V from CORNELLÀ to Badalona but this idea had been abandoned when the project was resumed in the early 1990s. Therefore trains coming from SAGRADA FAMÍLIA have to take a very tight turn to the right and then left again before arriving at ENCANTS. The rest of the alignment is quite straight. CLOT station was constructed diagonally under L1 platforms, which provides quite easy and fast transfer. Between the L2 platforms a wall was built to support the L1 station above. At LA PAU the L4 PEP VENTURA platform can be reached via one flight of stairs. Whereas the first stations on L2 all look very similar in design (mainly greyish materials), these five new stations, which were designed by different architects, look quite different from each other. Three are definitely among the more appealing stations on the Barcelona metro. ENCANTS looks similar to the older ones but is in a salmon tone, while CLOT is blue. BAC DE RODA has original bench designs and its peculiar vaulted roof looks like an upturned boat, flat at the ends and curved in the middle. SANT MARTÍ has a blue vaulted roof which is illuminated by huge light wedges. The last station LA PAU is also salmon coloured with a peculiar construction that supports the illumination.

The 2001–2010 infrastructure plan still includes the connection of L2 to the PEP VENTURA branch of L4, and to do so the system of current collection is being adapted. L2 is now 8.1km long and has 12 stations, six provide transfer to other lines and *RENFE* (PG. DE GRÀCIA and CLOT).

After the never-ending discussions during the early 1990s whether to extend L2 to Montjuïc and which other lines should be built, in spring 1997 finally the Barcelona Transport Authority was founded, which from now on should decide, plan and co-ordinate all public transit in the metropolitan area. While a new master plan was being prepared, the Generalitat decided to initiate two minor extensions which had been planned for years. The first included one more station on L4, which was made possible after building a new depot for L2 and L4 at the so-called *Triangle Ferroviari* (Railway triangle) between SANT ANDREU and LA PAU. L4 had used a depot beyond its ROQUETES terminus which could now be rebuilt into an extension to TRINITAT NOVA. Construction began in August 1998 and was scheduled to be concluded in December 1999, in time for the metro's 75th birthday. After the delays on L2, the Catalan government wanted to open this station even before its initial schedule, namely by the middle of October, just before the elections for the Catalan government, but after the finished

L2 LA PAU – a peculiar structure supporting the lights reminds us of the industrial past of the area. From here L2 trains will run to PEP VENTURA in Badalona in the future.

L4 Trinitat Nova – 1000-series train in original livery at Barcelona's newest metro station which was built after the former train depot was moved to the railway triangle in Sant Andreu.

section was handed over to the city owned metro company, they needed some weeks for trials and tests which caused some political polemics before the elections. Eventually the new station opened to the public without any inaugural celebration on 27 October 1999. Trinitat Nova is some 700m from Roquetes which was renamed into Via Júlia.

The new station looks very much like the 1995 L2 stations, but is peculiar as far as accesses are concerned. Due to its location along a slope under Aiguablava street, the northern exit to Pedrosa street is one level down from the platform. This is also the first station to use access doors (like in Paris) instead of the traditional turnstiles. Certain indications, such as 'Way in', 'Exit', 'Tickets' and directions are given in Catalan, Spanish and also in English. In the future, L3 is also planned to arrive at Trinitat Nova. There will be a new station called Roquetes, closer to the neighbourhood of that name, between Canyelles and this station.

L4 Trinitat Nova – due to its peculiar location the lift and escalator take passengers up to the platform from Pedrosa street entrance (on opening day 27 October 1999 when everything was still shiny).

Construction of a L3 extension from MONTBAU to CANYELLES had been a promise during election campaigns for some years. Before the Olympic Games a ring motorway which had been designed in the 1960s was built. Although this was a very good moment for construction in Barcelona, nothing was done for the metro in that area. The new extension will run under the side lanes of this main artery for about half of its length. Eventually construction began in March 1999 and it is mostly built by cut-and-cover using a vaulted roof. The new 2.4km section will have three stations, MUNDET which will mainly serve the university campus there and the Velòdrom stadium, VALLDAURA and CANYELLES. This section, which together with the L4 extension to TRINITAT NOVA is financed by the 1998–2000 investment contract totalling 45,000 million pesetas (of which one third is paid by the state and two thirds by the Catalan government), is scheduled to open in 2001. It will serve some 45,000 people living in the area and a total of 9million passengers a year are expected.

OTHER RAIL TRANSPORT IN AND AROUND BARCELONA

For railway and urban transit fans, Barcelona is a very interesting place to visit. Three different rail companies operate a dense network, using three different gauges. Most of these lines run underground within the city limits. The city also operates three funiculars, two cable cars, some open-air escalators and a vintage tramway. In a few years a modern tram line will complete this diversity.

Renfe Rodalies / Cercanías

As in Madrid, *RENFE* runs a network of four suburban lines around Barcelona. During the last 10–15 years the service has improved a lot, and accordingly ridership has risen significantly. All four lines cross the city in two north – south tunnels meeting at the main railway station BARCELONA-SANTS: C–1 (MAÇANET-MASSANES – BLANES – MATARÓ – Barcelona – L'HOSPITALET / AEROPORT), C–3 (VIC – Barcelona – L'HOSPITALET) and C–4 (MANRESA – TERRASSA – SABADELL – Barcelona – MARTORELL – VILAFRANCA – ST.VICENÇ DE CALDERS) use the tunnel via CLOT-ARAGÓ, ARC DE TRIOMF and PLAÇA CATALUNYA (PL. CATALUNYA – SANTS opened 1979), only C–2 (SANT VICENÇ DE CALDERS – SITGES – Barcelona – GRANOLLERS – SANT CELONI) uses the tunnel under Aragó street via PASSEIG DE GRÀCIA. This line was originally built in a trench in 1882, as a link between the old Sants station and the Estació de França (some time ago also called Término). In 1902 a station was established at PASSEIG DE GRÀCIA, and in

C2 VILANOVA I LA GELTRÚ – 447-series units on sidetracks. This station is the terminus for some trains on the C2 suburban service. Along this busy corridor, *RENFE* tracks are used by local, long distance and freight trains. The Railway Museum is next to the station.

An FGC 112-series train at the Pl. Catalunya terminus, ready to depart for Sabadell on an S2 service on the *Metro del Vallès* network. Suburban lines skip some stations on the urban stretch of the line (Sant Gervasi, Bonanova, Tres Torres).

Plaça d'Espanya – entrance to the underground Barcelona terminus of the *Metro del Baix Llobregat*, which will be extended to Pl. Francesc Macià and Gràcia in the future. The L1 station lies to the left, in front of the former bull ring and the L3 station is on the right under Paral.lel Avenue. The view is along Gran Via towards the city centre, which can also be reached via a road tunnel under the square.

1960, most of this link line was covered. In 1975, a single-track line was built from Sants to the airport (now part of line C–1, 30-minute interval). Both city tunnels are also used by regional and long distance trains. In the Vallès area there is a link line only used by freight trains between El Papiol (on line C–4 south) and Cerdanyola (C–4 north) via Sant Cugat, which might be used for passenger service in the future. A few years ago a C–4 branch from Cerdanyola to Universitat Autònoma was put into service. The future line could operate as a ring line (Sants – Sant Feliu de Ll. – Molins de Rei – Rubí – Sant Cugat AVE – Cerdanyola – Sagrera – Sants) and serve the *AVE* high-speed train station planned in that area. There are also plans to build a third cross-city tunnel along Mallorca and Provença streets for suburban services, and to reserve the Aragó tunnel for the new *AVE* high-speed train link due to be operating by 2004 (with a second main station at Sagrera).

Rodalies trains operate at irregular intervals, approximately every 10–30 minutes on C–1, C–2 and C–4 and every 20–40 minutes on C–3 according to the time of the day and the distance from Barcelona. To increase travel speed, not all trains stop at all stations outside Barcelona. The last trains leave Barcelona at around 23.00h. Direct transfer to the metro is provided at CORNELLÀ (L5), L'HOSPITALET (L1 JUST OLIVERAS), SANTS (L3, L5), PLAÇA CATALUNYA (L1, L3, U6, U7), PASSEIG DE GRÀCIA (L2, L3, L4), ARC DE TRIOMF (L1), CLOT ARAGÓ (L1, L2) and SANT ANDREU ARENAL (L1 FABRA I PUIG); SANT ANDREU COMTAL is within walking distance of SANT ANDREU metro station (L1).

C–1 includes Spain's first railway built from Barcelona to MATARÓ (1848), although the section between Barcelona (Estació de França) and SANT ADRIÀ DE BESÒS was dismantled in the late 1980s in order to build the Olympic Village and the Poblenou Park.

Ferrocarrils de la Generalitat de Catalunya (FGC)

Metro del Baix Llobregat

The first of today's *FGC* lines (these lines were handed over to the Catalan government in 1979) was the Martorell – Igualada line, which opened in 1892 (but which was the last one to be electrified in 1998). The 29km long line from Barcelona-Magòria to Martorell followed in 1912. This network, which was extended to Manresa and further north to Súria during the 1920s, uses metre gauge. In 1926, a branch line was built towards the harbour, and a 1km long single-track tunnel to link the line to the new Metro Transversal at PLAÇA ESPANYA. During the 1980s the line was put underground as far as CORNELLÀ-RIERA (11km) and its alignment was changed to serve more areas within the city of L'Hospitalet (the original alignment can be seen on city maps along Avinguda Carrilet). After the station CORNELLÀ-RIERA the line comes to the surface and crosses the River Llobregat on a bridge before arriving at SANT BOI, from where it follows the river all the way to MANRESA (via Montserrat which is served by a cable-car directly from the AERI DE MONTSERRAT stop).

Since the mid-1990s, the formerly called *CATALANS* line has been converted into the so-called *METRO DEL BAIX LLOBREGAT*. Therefore the terminus station at PLAÇA ESPANYA was expanded from two to four tracks and an intermediate station was built at MAGÒRIA-LA CAMPANA. The double track section was extended from MOLÍ NOU via the new station at SANTA COLOMA DE CERVELLÓ (the former station with that name was also rebuilt and renamed COLÒNIA GÜELL) to CAN ROS. In order to further increase frequencies as far as OLESA DE MONTSERRAT, the line will be put underground on its way through PALLEJÀ and SANT ANDREU DE LA BARCA, and another station will be built at Quatre Camins (after SANT VICENÇ DELS HORTS) with large park-and-ride facilities. New trains (213-series), which have a low-floor section for easy wheel-chair access, were bought to replace the old diesel units that ran on the Igualada branch. During the last 20 years, more than 200 level crossings could be eliminated, leaving only 17 along the lines served by passenger trains.

In 2000, the *METRO DEL BAIX LLOBREGAT* offers a 7.5 minute service between PLAÇA ESPANYA and MOLÍ NOU (S3), a train every 15 minutes to CAN ROS (S33) and every 30 minutes to MARTORELL (S8) and OLESA DE MONTSERRAT (S4), plus an hourly service on the regional lines to MANRESA and IGUALADA (R5, R6 only stopping at major stations between Barcelona and MARTORELL). PLAÇA ESPANYA and L'HOSPITALET-AV. CARRILET (L1) offer easy transfer between the *METRO DEL BAIX LLOBREGAT* and the Barcelona Metro. This Y-shaped network is 99km long and carried some 11million people in 1999.

Metro del Vallès

The origin of this line was described together with the history of the metro, as from its beginning it has had a rather urban character between Barcelona (PLAÇA CATALUNYA) and SARRIÀ. Although originally built using Spanish gauge (1672mm), it was changed to international gauge in 1905 in order to allow its future direct connection to the French railway network (a dream which has never come true). From SARRIÀ, a tunnel was built under the Collserola mountain and the line arrived at SANT CUGAT in 1917. There the line splits into two branches, the first to TERRASSA (1919) and the second to SABADELL-RAMBLA (1922). This double-track network has a total length of 43km. In the 1980s, the terminus at TERRASSA was put underground and closer to the city centre, and a branch was built from

BELLATERRA to the campus of the UNIVERSITAT AUTÒNOMA. In 1996, this branch was extended into a loop so that all S2 trains to SABADELL-RAMBLA can serve the university directly. In that year a service began under the name of *METRO DEL VALLÈS*, offering a train every 6 minutes between Barcelona and SANT CUGAT (S5) and every 12–15 minutes to TERRASSA (S1) and SABADELL (S2) from 05:00 until around midnight (until later on weekends). Urban services were also given numbers, U6 to REINA ELISENDA and U7 to AV. TIBIDABO (now also referred to as *Línia de Balmes*).

Tramvia Blau

Until 1971, Barcelona had a very extensive tramway network. But, like in so many other cities, trams had become a nuisance for the motor car and were eventually withdrawn from the city's streets. The only reminder of this glorious past is the *TRAMVIA BLAU* (the blue tram), which still connects the *FGC* AV. TIBIDABO station to the ground station of the Tibidabo Funicular. Today it is mainly a tourist attraction, rising almost as steeply as San Francisco's famous streetcars.

Funiculars, cable cars and escalators

There are three existing funicular railways: 1 – *FUNICULAR DE VALLVIDRERA* is an important urban transport link. Leaving from right on top of the *FGC* PEU DEL FUNICULAR station it serves the village of Vallvidrera situated on the Collserola mountain. It was built in 1906 and totally renovated in 1998. It also helps to reach the Tibidabo leisure park, together with 2 – *TIBIDABO FUNICULAR*. 3 – *MONTJUÏC FUNICULAR*, which was entirely rebuilt for the 1992 Olympic Games, acting as the only other option to climbing the mountain where the Olympic stadium and pavilion are located. Unfortunately it only operates during weekends and vacation periods. It starts underground close to the PARAL.LEL metro station.

The upper end of the *MONTJUÏC FUNICULAR* is directly connected to the Montjuïc cable car, which takes visitors up to the fortress in small cabins within a few minutes. The intermediate stop at the Montjuïc leisure park is out of service. The second cable car is also a tourist attraction. It spans high over the old harbour between Montjuïc mountain and the Barceloneta beach.

As the metro didn't reach the mountain of Montjuïc in time for the Olympic Games, the city decided to improve access by a flight of open-air escalators which start near PLAÇA ESPANYA and climb up the mountain close to Palau Nacional. There are more open-air escalators near metro station VALLCARCA along the steep street Baixada de les Glòries that also leads up to Gaudí's Parc Güell.

BARCELONA METRO – OPERATION AND FARE SYSTEM

On weekdays the Barcelona Metro operates every 4–6 minutes from 5:00 until 23:00. On Fridays, Saturdays and the day before a public holiday, service is extended until 2:00. On Sundays and other holidays trains run from 6:00 until 24:00 at longer intervals.

Until 1993, there was no season ticket available for public transport in Barcelona. After a trial period during the 1992 Olympic Games, a monthly pass was eventually introduced in February 1993, valid for city buses, metro and *FGC* trains within the city boundaries (only on the Sarrià / Tibidabo Line). This ticket (the first of the magnetic credit card size tickets) complemented the traditional basic offer of single tickets, the T–1 (10 rides) strip card which was valid for buses, metro or *FGC* trains (without transfer between any of these) and the T–2 (10 rides) strip card only for metro or *FGC* trains (slightly cheaper than the T–1).

The monthly pass was never as popular as the *Abono de Transporte* in Madrid, mainly because its price has been too high for people who use public transport only twice a day to get to work or school.

When the Metropolitan Transport Authority (*Autoritat del Transport Metropolità –ATM*) was finally born in 1997, first efforts were made to reach full integration of tariffs not only within the city of Barcelona but within its extended metropolitan area populated by some 4million people.

L4 TRINITAT NOVA – sliding doors were installed here for the first time instead of turnstiles and tickets have to be introduced in the machine to the right instead of the traditional left. Although far from tourist areas, signs are also now written in English.

L3 FONTANA – the refurbished ticket hall is the only one at street level. Three flights of escalators lead down to platform level.

From January 1998, T–1 and T–2 tickets could also be used on all *FGC* trains within the municipalities also served by the metro, i.e. as far as LES PLANES on the Vallès lines (including the *FUNICULAR DE VALLVIDRERA*) and to CORNELLÀ-RIERA on the Baix Llobregat lines, with free transfer between these trains and the metro.

During early 1999, validating machines for magnetic tickets were also installed in all city buses and eventually the T–2 ticket was abolished, which leaves the T–1 ticket as the most popular.

From the beginning of 2000 monthly passes can also be used on *RENFE* commuter trains within Zone 1 of the future zonal system.

During the last years other tickets have been available which will be listed below.

In April 2000, the *ATM* announced that from January 2001 Barcelona and its extended metropolitan area (covering distances of up to 70km as far as Vic, Igualada or Blanes) will have an integrated tariff system with six zones for all means of transport operating in the area, suburban and local buses, *FGC* and *RENFE* trains and metro.

Tickets

available in the year 2000 (prices shown in € – Euro):

Senzill	Single ticket – no transfer	€0.90
T–1	(10 rides with transfer between metro and FGC trains)	€4.96
T–Mes	(monthly pass)	€33.43
T–4	(10 rides for the elderly)	€2.16
T–50/30	(50 rides within 30 days)	€20.18
T–10x2	(10 rides on metro/FGC trains plus transfer to TMB buses)	€7.98
T–Dia	(1-Day Pass)	€3.76
3–Dies	(3-Day Pass) – not valid on FGC trains	€8.71
5–Dies	(5-Day Pass) – not valid on FGC trains	€12.92

There are also combined monthly passes for people travelling on *FGC* trains from outside Zone 1 with transfer to the metro. Another special offer is a day's or a week's car parking at GLÒRIES car park including a daily or weekly pass. The airport bus also sells 3- and 5-day passes at a special rate.

Among all metros in Spain, Barcelona definitely has the nicest tickets, worth becoming a collector's item. The credit card size tickets carry a different image every few weeks commemorating some event. Monthly passes have been the same since they were introduced in 1993 showing six different images, symbols of the 1992 Barcelona when lots of areas had been redeveloped for the Olympic Games.

Tickets can be bought from automatic vending machines (newer ones also accept bills and credit cards) or from the ticket offices (at least one manned entrance per station). Tickets have to be introduced into validating machines to release the turnstiles. TRINITAT NOVA and the *RENFE* PLAÇA CATALUNYA station have been equipped with platform access doors, like the ones existing in Valencia or Paris.

In 1998, the Barcelona Metro carried 281 million passengers. This number rose to 286.7million during 1999. *FERROCARRILS DE LA GENERALITAT DE CATALUNYA* (*FGC*) added some 44.5million passengers within the central zone of the metropolitan area (covering an approximately 20km radius). According to statistics published by the *ATM*, *RENFE* Rodalies transported 37.8 million people within this area. Outside the central zone, another 12.4 million people used *FGC* trains and 52.3million rode on a *RENFE* suburban train. The strongest increase, compared to 1998, was for *FGC* within the central zone, mainly due to better integration of their urban sections into the metro network, converting both Vallès and Baix Llobregat trains into just another metro line.

Trains sometimes carry full adverts like this one for the celebration of FC Barcelona's 100th birthday, sponsored by a mobile phone company.

BARCELONA METRO – ROLLING STOCK

The Barcelona Metro is served by two quite different generations of trains, that of the 1000/1100-series introduced in the 1970s and operating on L4 and L5, and newer trains of the 2000/3000/4000-series running on L1, L2 and L3 which were gradually introduced between 1986 and 1997. On all lines 5-car trains are used, which fit to the standard 90m long platforms. Although all trains are equipped with pantographs and with third rail power collectors, only L2 and L5 have always been using overhead power supply. A rigid catenary was installed for the first time on L2. This system is now being extended to all other lines. Air-conditioning, acoustic and visual station announcement is installed in all newer trains, whilst most older trains have been refitted with air-conditioning. Trains on L5 also offer acoustic station announcement.

1000-series

The first 50 units were ordered in 1966 to start service on the new L5 (initially only 2-car trains were used). They were produced by Maquinista and Macosa, two Barcelona-based companies now part of Alstom, and started operation between 1970 and 1976. Later another 108 units of the 1100-series plus 52 trailers were ordered to cover needs on the new L4 and also on L3 (on the then IIIB section). These were also equipped with a third rail power collector and were put into service between 1974 and 1979. Originally painted dark blue and light blue with white stripes, some trains have come back from a general overhaul recently in a complete pale grey livery, which makes them look unfinished. The original interior in light green with purple benches has also been changed to black and white, similar to trains on L1–L3. Today there are 260 carriages (including 52 trailers) of this series in operation.

Above The original interior of the 1000-series boasts a typical 1970s colour scheme in purple and light green. Enough space is provided for standing passengers, but with only few poles to hold on to.

Right A repainted 1000-series unit on the short surface stretch near the Can Boixeres depot on L5. The picture is taken from the covered station.

3000/4000-series

A total of 42 of these trains were ordered from CAF and Maquinista between 1984 and 1988 and they drastically changed the image of the Barcelona Metro by replacing up to 60 years old and, especially in the summer, very uncomfortable rolling stock.

All trains consist of five cars (including four motor-cars and one trailer). The difference between both series is basically the gauge – 3000-series have international gauge (L3) and 4000-series trains can only run on L1 which has Spanish gauge (1672mm). Whereas all other metro cars are 2.71m wide, the 4000-series trains have a width of 3.1m and thus offer notably more space.

These trains are fed by 1500Vdc whereas the rest of the lines has 1200Vdc. All cars are 17m long and have four doors on each side which can be opened individually by the passengers. At each end of the car, an arrow indicates the side of the next station's platform, a quite useful service on L1, not so much on L3 which has only side platforms. These trains started operation between 1986 and 1990. Today there are 90 cars of the 3000-series (18 trailers) and 120 of the 4000-series (24 trailers).

Trains of the 4000-series operating on L1 are 3.1m wide due to Spanish standard gauge (1672mm) on this line.

2000-series

These trains were ordered from CAF and Meinfesa in 1991 for the future L2. Although they are quite identical to those of the 3000-series on L3, they allow free movement between cars which helps to distribute passengers, but mainly improves the feeling of safety. As the inauguration of L2 was delayed until 1995, the first 3-car trains delivered in 1992 were put in service on L3 together with two cars of the 3000-series. Apart from small differences in design (front window, seats, etc.), these trains have a reserved space for wheelchairs next to the driver's cabin. Between 1995 and 1997 they operated as 3-car trains on the short L2 from PARAL.LEL to SAGRADA FAMÍLIA. From September 1997 5-car trains have been running all the way to LA PAU. Today there are 55 cars of the 2000-series (11 trailers) operating on L2, although one train runs on L3.

Left For L2 a new type of trains was ordered which allows passengers to walk freely from one end to the other (2000-series). One of these trains is in use on L3.

Below The 2000-series were the first trains in Barcelona to be operated in ATO mode and although a third rail can be seen here, power supply is via a rigid overhead line, a system which is now extended to all other lines. L2 PARAL.LEL station allows the most comfortable transfer between L2 and L3 (the platform in direction ZONA UNIVERSITÀRIA is just behind the wall on the right).

Ferrocarrils de la Generalitat de Catalunya

The *FGC* also runs trains with two different gauges, 1000mm on the *BAIX LLOBREGAT* network, and international gauge on the *VALLÈS* network. For the metro-like section of this network (U6, U7) trains of the 111-series are used, 20 of which were delivered from 1983 on. A standard 3-car train is 60m long and 2.75m wide. Tension on these lines is 1500Vdc and overhead power collection is used. As these trains are also used on the suburban branches of the network, they were designed to be slightly more comfortable than most standard metro cars, with brown upholstered seats. Since 1995, 16 trains of a new 112-series have replaced older rolling stock (partly sold to Cuba), which are 80m long. These new trains, the most comfortable ones running in and around Barcelona, operate on S1 and S2 to SABADELL and TERRASSA.

Left The 112-series is the newest rolling stock in service on the *Metro del Vallès*, the *FGC* suburban service, which operates a metro-like timetable with trains every 6 minutes to Sant Cugat.

Below A 213-series unit at the newly built Santa Coloma de Cervelló station on a *Metro del Baix Llobregat* service (May 2000). These new trains have a low floor access in the middle of the train.

On the *Baix Llobregat* network (750V) a variant of the 111-series, the 211-series, is used, although electric (5000-series) and diesel (3000-series) trains also ran until recently. Ten 3-car and five 2-car trains of the 211-series started operation between 1987 and 1988. Stations along this network have low platforms, therefore access to trains is difficult, especially for people in wheelchairs or with prams. This problem was partly solved with the acquisition of 20 new 3-car trains of the 213-series (50.4m long) which have a low-floor section in the middle.

BARCELONA METRO - PROJECTS FOR 2010

In the summer of 1999, the *ATM* (Metropolitan Transport Authority) finally approved an ambitious master plan (*Plan director d'infraestructures* – PDI) for the period 2001–2010, which includes all necessary action to improve public transport in the Barcelona metropolitan area. Although all different administrations and major transport operators are represented in the *ATM*, only the future will show whether all projects will be carried out within the established time frame. This master plan defines a significant expansion of the existing metro network, plus the construction of a new line. In addition to that there will be improvements to the *RENFE* suburban rail service, major projects for *FGC* lines within Barcelona and the construction of a modern tram network in and around Barcelona.

1. Metro Extension Projects

L1 will be extended at both ends, in the north from FONDO to Badalona Centre (L2) via Montigalà, Lloreda, Sant Crist and Bufalà (three or four intermediate stations), and in the south from FEIXA LLARGA to El Prat de Llobregat (two or three stations).

L2 will continue, as originally planned, from LA PAU to PEP VENTURA, instead of L4, and then run further north to Badalona Centre (L1) and Morera (three or four new stations). At the other end it might eventually be extended from SANT ANTONI to Passeig de la Zona Franca and the Pedrosa Fairgrounds (L9) via POBLE SEC and Montjuïc.

L3 will be extended from its 2001 terminus at CANYELLES to TRINITAT NOVA (one intermediate station at Roquetes).

L4 will be extended from LA PAU to the planned Sagrera *AVE* Railway Station (L9). For this extension a tunnel leading to the depot at *Triangle Ferroviari* can partly be used. There might be an intermediate station at the crossroads of Santander Street and Rambla del Prim. At the other end, from TRINITAT NOVA to Ciutat Meridiana and Can Cuiàs, a light metro will be built (decision taken in early 2000). This will be a separate single track underground line with double track at stations to allow crossing of trains. Although light rail vehicles will be used initially, the tunnel will be built to full metro standards so it can be upgraded later if considered necessary.

L5 will finally reach VALL D'HEBRON (L3) via Carmel and Teixonera-Coll. All three new stations will be among the deepest of the Barcelona metro network, due to the mountainous relief of the area. Whereas Carmel and VALL D'HEBRON will lie some 30–40m deep, Teixonera-Coll will be 70m underground. Here an inclined elevator parallel to the escalators is planned. This extension might open in 2003.

L9 The new Line 9 will be semicircular and connect all other metro and rail lines along its route. The definite alignment was decided upon in June 2000 and the line will most likely be opened in various stages. EU funds have been

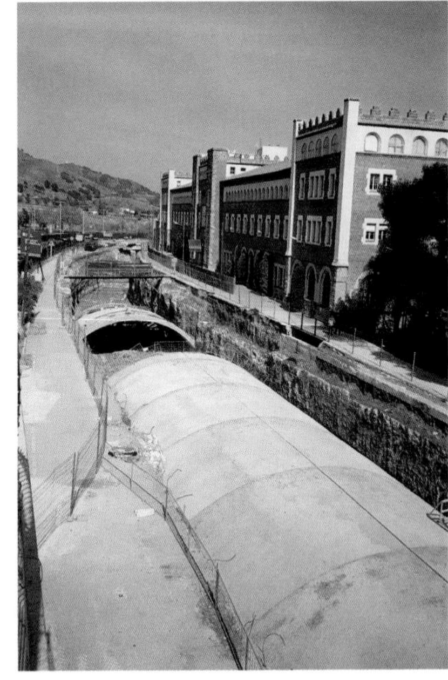

L3 – Construction was well underway between MUNDET and VALLDAURA in April 2000 on the extension to CANYELLES due to open during 2001. A vaulted roof just below street level was chosen for this section. Here the line follows the side lanes of the city's ring motorway built for the 1992 Olympics.

applied for in order to help with the financing of this ambitious project. The new 35km long line will start at the airport and run through the Zona Franca industrial area. It will also provide service for the Barcelona Trade Fair 2 at Pedrosa, then follow Passeig de la Zona Franca and intersect with Metro del Baix Llobregat at Ildefons Cerdà. The next interchange will be with L1 between Torrassa and Santa Eulàlia, which will also offer transfer to all *Renfe* Rodalies lines. Transfer to L5 will be at Collblanc and after Camp Nou, the FC Barcelona Football Stadium, it will meet L3 at Zona Universitària and Maria Cristina. L9 will continue its way uphill to Sarrià (U6 and Metro del Vallès), although a new interchange station might be built by merging Sarrià and Tres Torres stations, which are quite close to each other. From here the line will turn right and run parallel to the sea, crossing U7 (Línia de Balmes) at El Putxet. L3 will have another transfer station to L9 at Lesseps. The first interchange to L4 will be Guinardó before L9 arrives at the current Sagrera station situated on Meridiana Avenue. When the new Sagrera *AVE* Railway Station was designed for the first time some ten years earlier, a shuttle metro was planned between the railway station and Sagrera metro station. Now this section will be covered by L9. Sagrera *AVE* will also provide a link to L4 then extended from La Pau. After this new main station, L9 will run northeast to Bon Pastor and under the Besòs river where it will split up into two branches, one to Santa Coloma (Singuerlín) and one to Badalona (Gorg – L2).

Apart from these new extensions, the metro network will be improved by adding new stations in badly served areas. Two more stations could be built along L4, one at Virrei Amat between Llucmajor and Maragall and another one at Diagonal-Mar between Selva de Mar and Besòs Mar where a new residential area and a shopping centre is being developed. Another additional station might be in the neighbourhood of Sant Feliu between Collblanc and Pubilla Cases on L5.

2. FGC Extensions

After an important upgrading of the *Metro del Baix Llobregat* during the late 1990s, this line will be extended from its traditional terminus at Plaça Espanya towards more areas in central Barcelona, and become line U8. A first stage will lead to Plaça Francesc Macià (Trambaix) via Hospital Clínic (L5). Later it will meet the *FGC Metro del Vallès* either at Gràcia or Muntaner. Due to different gauge and tunnel profiles both networks cannot, however, be connected.

Some time ago an option was discussed to convert the Tibidabo branch to metre gauge and connect it to the *Metro del Baix Llobregat* network. But more recent plans study the possibility of creating a loop for *Metro del Vallès* and Tibidabo trains thus avoiding the cul-de-sac at Plaça Catalunya. Instead of terminating there, trains would run around the square and along Passeig de Gràcia (parallel to L3). They would eventually come back to Gràcia station. The loop would include two major transfer stations, one at Passeig de Gràcia (L3 and future *AVE*) and at Diagonal (L3, L5 and future *Renfe* Rodalies station).

Outside Barcelona city, in Terrassa, an underground extension will be built to Can Roca, including three stations, one of which will be directly connected to Terrassa *Renfe* station (which was also put underground in the mid-1990s).

A long, and usually crowded, transfer corridor links L1 and L3 platforms at Espanya. All platforms and corridors have video surveillance.

L1 URGELL entrance on Gran Via, a typical '*boca de metro*' (metro mouth). The panel on the street includes the name of the station, the lines serving it and a network map.

Another important extension outside Barcelona would be a *METRO DEL BAIX LLOBREGAT* branch from SANT BOI to Castelldefels via Viladecans and Gavà, areas now only served by the *RENFE* C–2 line, with stations sometimes too far from the urban centres, especially in VILADECANS. Whereas local governments defend a full metro for this corridor, the Catalan government seems to be in favour of a light rail solution.

3. Renfe suburban network improvements

The PDI is examining a better connection to the airport, either by extending one or more metro lines and/or by diverting the *RENFE* C–2 route to VILANOVA-LA GELTRÚ via the airport terminal. A decision for the *AVE* high speed route is also to be taken soon. As described in the section 'Other Railways in and around Barcelona', a circular or tangential line should be established by using an existing freight line between MOLLET – CERDANYOLA – SANT CUGAT and PAPIOL. The route to VIC (C–3) should be double tracked between MONTCADA and LA GARRIGA to allow higher frequencies.

4. Tram network

After awarding contracts to Alstom to build the initial section of the Trambaix from Pl. Francesc Macià to Esplugues, Cornellà and St. Joan Despí, studies are being carried out for a route through the centre of Barcelona along Diagonal avenue. Whereas the north-eastern section between GLÒRIES and the sea front will run on street level, the middle section might as well be underground. Diagonal avenue is narrower along this section and has too many street intersections with dense traffic on most crossing streets. Even if a perfect control system gave priority to the trams, this system would gridlock car traffic in a large area of Barcelona.

5. Plaça Catalunya transfer hub

In order to improve transfer facilities between different means of transport in the Barcelona city centre around Plaça Catalunya, projects are being considered to create a huge interchange station which includes an area limited by URQUINAONA (L1, L4), PASSEIG DE GRÀCIA (L2, L3, L4, *RENFE*), UNIVERSITAT (L1, L2) and the lower part of PLAÇA CATALUNYA (L3, FGC) with another L1 and *RENFE* station in between on PLAÇA CATALUNYA. This area is used by some 500,000 passengers a day, who either change lines here or have the central shopping district as their final destination.

VALENCIA METRO

INTRODUCTION

Valencia is Spain's third largest city (800,000 inhabitants with over a million in the metropolitan area). It lies 350km east of Madrid and 350km south of Barcelona by the Mediterranean Sea, and is the capital of the *Comunitat Valenciana* (one of Spain's 17 autonomous regions) which comprises the provinces of Castelló de la Plana, Valencia and Alicante (Alacant). Like Catalonia this is a bilingual region, with both Spanish (also called Castilian) and Valencian (the southern variant of Catalan) as official languages. Whereas in Catalonia only Catalan names are officially used for towns, streets, stations and other place names, in Valencia there is a mixed usage in everyday life. Maps show names in Spanish or Valencian, or both, although there is a certain tendency to use Valencian spelling, which in many cases only differs by some written accents from its Spanish counterpart (for example Spanish Valencia or Turia, and Valencian València and Túria). In this book names are

Rail transit in the metropolitan area of Valencia as operated in the year 2000 and with future plans.

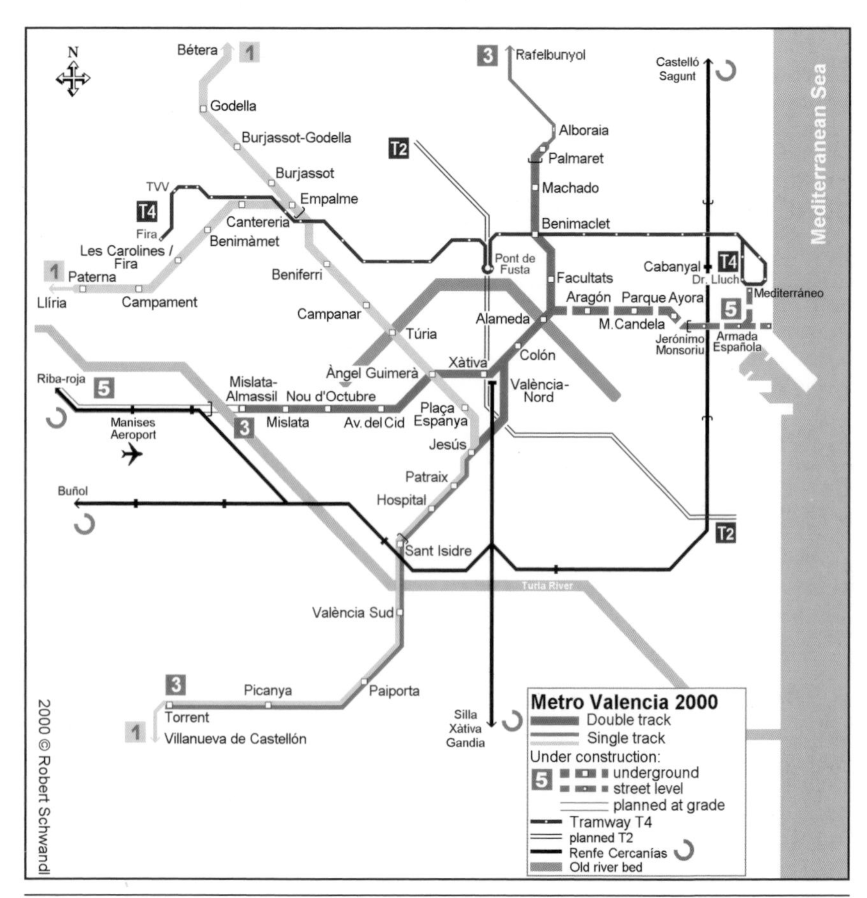

A repainted 3700-series train at CARLET on the southern branch of Line 1. Behind is one of the nicest original station buildings dating back to the end of the 19th century.

used as shown on official metro or city maps (although they even vary here according to the edition, like Alboraya –Alboraia, Vilanova de Castelló – Villanueva de Castellón, etc).

The Valencia metro is not a metro or subway in the classical sense of the word. As you will read in the following chapter, it was developed out of a suburban network and today it has two very different faces. One that is the continuation of the original lines opened in 1888, with trains running between orange and lemon trees and serving small villages that have become dormitory towns over the last decades. Along these rural sections of the network there are still many level-crossings, and at some stations along Line 1 passengers have to press a button or wave their arm so that the train stops. Unfortunately some sections on this line look very abandonded and the tracks are also in a poor state.

The other face is a very modern urban underground metro network which in its own right deserves being in this book. Depending on the definition of what a real metro is, one could say that Line 1 between EMPALME and VALÈNCIA-SUD and Line 3 between MISLATA-ALMASSIL and PALMARET are real metro lines as they are totally independent from other traffic, absolutely urban, mostly underground and they operate at an interval of 4–7 minutes during the week and 10 minutes in the evenings and at weekends. Using these criteria, the metro network would be approximately 18km long (16.3km underground) with 22 stations (18 underground).

If the definition allows some level crossings, metro transit on Line 1 could be extended as far as TORRENT in the south (double track and a basic 7.5min interval), and to PATERNA or SEMINARI in the north (double track and 15 minutes headway), as the trains serve an almost continuously built-up area along these routes.

Valencia also stands for tram revival in Spain, since the first modern tramway line was put into service, some 25 years after all tramway routes in Spain had been closed.

Apart from the Metro Valencia run by *FERROCARRILS DE LA GENERALITAT VALENCIANA*, Valencia also has a suburban service run by *RENFE*. There are five *CERCANÍAS* lines, C1–C4 and C6 (C5 only offers one train a day!), radiating from València-Nord operating at a basic 30 minute interval with mixed traffic along the *RENFE* mainline routes. Lines C–3 and C–4 are served by diesel trains.

VALENCIA METRO – HISTORY AND FUTURE

By the end of the 19th century, Valencia had a population of about 215,000. At that time tramways had appeared on the streets of all major Spanish cities, first drawn by horses and eventually being electrified. Valencia had also become one of Spain's most important sea ports, although unlike Barcelona or Vigo its port lies some 5km from the city centre. Limited by the Mediterranean Sea to the east, the city is surrounded by the Horta de Valencia in the north, west and south, which are quite plain agricultural lands growing mainly fruit and vegetables. The whole area was spread with little

Left At the northern terminus of Line 3, Rafelbunyol, platforms were elevated to improve access to modern cars. Therefore the original station building is now on a lower level than the platforms. This peculiar situation can be seen at many surface stations.

Facing page A Babcock-Wilcox train is arriving at Empalme from the city tunnel, heading for Llíria. On the left, tracks to Bétera can be seen and on the right is the reserved right-of-way for tram T4. To improve connections, the new Empalme station is under construction in the background.

farmers' villages, which needed to be connected to the capital and its port by the new means of transport, the railway. Both the *Compañía de Ferrocarriles del Norte* and the *MZA* (*Ferrocarriles de Madrid a Zaragoza y Alicante*) had reached Valencia by 1854 using Spanish standard gauge (1672mm). For the local railways serving the rural areas around Valencia, the metre-gauge was chosen and concession to build and operate four lines of a *Ferrocarril económico* in the north of Valencia was granted to the tramway operator *Sociedad Valenciana de Tranvías*.

The first of the four lines opened in 1888 and ran between Valencia and Liria. The terminal station in Valencia was built at Marxalenes. Initially the 27km line had only eight stations (which are still visible today on the Llíria branch of L–1): Marxalenes (now on T4), Burjassot (now Empalme), Paterna, Pla, L'Eliana, Pobla de Vallbona, Benaguasil and Liria (in Valencian spelled Llíria).

Three years later, in 1891, a branch was added from Empalme to Bétera (14.7km) with stops at Burjassot-Godella, Godella, Rocafort, Massarojos, Montcada, Masies and Bétera. Later more stops were established along the two routes as villages kept growing.

In 1892 the original terminal station at Marxalenes was rebuilt and a new, more representative terminal building was erected closer to the old city centre of Valencia. As it was behind the church of Santa Monica it was referred to by this name, although officially its name was Estación Central de Valencia. Soon a wooden foot bridge was built across the Turia river and the station became popularly known by the name of Pont de Fusta or Puente de Madera which means 'wooden bridge'. Together with the new station, the third of the four planned lines was inaugurated, from Valencia – Pont de Fusta to El Grao (Valencia's harbour). This new connection would provide easy transport for the agricultural production from the Horta to the sea port and from there to the rest of the world. Apart from the goods transport, this line also had to fulfil a task of urban transport for some neighbourhoods in northeast Valencia. Along the 5.7km long route there were five intermediate stops which can still be recognised today along tram line T4: Benimaclet, La Carrasca, La Cadena, Les Termes and Les Arenes.

The last of the four northern lines was put into service only a few months later, in 1893. This line also had its Valencia terminus at Pont de Fusta and went northeast to Alboraia, Almàssara, Meliana, Foios, Albalat del Sorrels, Museros, Massamagrell and Rafelbunyol. This 13.3km line was initially planned to continue towards Sagunt and Segorbe, therefore Rafelbunyol was not built as a terminus station (like Bétera and Llíria), but the extension never became reality.

At the same time the Horta, south of Valencia, also felt the need for better transport towards Valencia and its harbour. The concession for the construction of one line was granted to the *Sociedad de Carbones Minerales de Dos Aguas y Ferrocarril del Grao de Valencia a Turís*, a small town west of Valencia which has never yet seen a train. The first section was opened in 1893 between

Valencia (Jesús) and Torrent with stops at Paiporta and Picanya (8.4km). One year later it reached Picassent and in 1895 Alberic. The eastern 5.5km long section between the Jesús terminus and the harbour started in 1912 but was mainly used for goods transport.

In 1917, the year in which this line was extended to Vilanova de Castelló (also called Castelló de la Ribera), the northern lines were integrated into the new *CTFV* (*Compañía de tranvías y ferrocarriles de Valencia*), which would eventually also own the southern line (1946). Two years later this company started electrifying all northern lines (finished by 1928) and laying double track on the busy route between Pont de Fusta and Empalme, which was used by trains running to Bétera and Llíria. In 1934, a project was designed to connect the northern lines to the southern line via a cross-city tunnel but, as in other Spanish cities, the beginning of the Spanish Civil War stopped all big construction projects. Following the war period, in 1941, a more detailed project for a rail link was planned, which included a 3.3km city tunnel starting at Pont de Fusta and running under the heart of the old city towards Jesús with stations along the route at Plaza de la Virgen (Cathedral), Calle de San Vicente, Plaza del Caudillo (now Plaça del País Valencià where the Town Hall is) and Gran Vía de Ramón y Cajal (close to today's Plaça d'Espanya station). Lack of funds postponed the project this time, which would be discussed again and again during the following decades.

In the late 1940s, after the *CTFV* had taken full responsibility of the southern line, electrification of this line began. On the northern lines the double track section was extended from Empalme to Paterna (1947), which allowed a more frequent service to the growing suburbs. In 1949, the original wooden bridge connecting the main terminus station to the city centre was destroyed by a flood and was totally rebuilt. In 1950 the line to Bétera was widened to double track as far as Seminari, which was opened as a new station. On the southern line another stop was added in the suburban area called Sant Isidre (which was nearer to where today's station Valencia-Sud is than the present Sant Isidre station). All lines had become very popular, in 1953 they carried 128million passengers. However, as in Madrid, the State didn't allow proper fare rises parallel to rising wages, so the apparently well running trains were not such a good business for the company.

On 14 October 1957 heavy floods destroyed many parts of Valencia and damage for the *CTFV* was enormous. The branch line from Jesús to Natzaret and the port was permanently closed, a lot of rolling stock and infrastructure had to be repaired. To avoid future disasters like this, the city decided to divert the river Turia into a new bed, bypassing the city in the south. The old river-bed became a long park right through the heart of the city.

As in many other parts of Spain, during the 1950s and 1960s there was a strong migration towards Valencia from many rural areas and southern Spain. The situation of the narrow gauge railway and tram company had become so bad that it could not cope with this population growth, neither by improving service nor by building new lines. In 1964, all urban and interurban tramway lines were taken over by the city, which meant that the company was left

JESÚS is a typical station along the city tunnel opened in 1988. The dark ceiling makes these stations look very low and unattractive compared to new stations on Line 3. This one can be distinguished by its yellow tiles along the lower part of the walls.

with the relatively less profitable local trains. The only way out of the situation was to hand them over to the State.

In 1941, all standard Spanish gauge lines all around the country were taken over by the State and integrated into *RENFE*. For narrow gauge lines the State had founded *FEVE* (*FERROCARRILES ESPAÑOLES DE VÍA ESTRECHA*), which operated lots of other lines mainly along the northern coast of Spain (see Bilbao section of this book). *FEVE* was responsible for the Valencia narrow gauge lines, as from 1 November 1964. State funding at least covered the grown deficit, but *FEVE* did not invest in new rolling stock until 1972. Trains were still very popular and very punctual, but very uncomfortable. From 1970 no goods were transported any longer, and finally some used trains were bought from the Belgian company *SNCV* (*SOCIÉTÉ NATIONALE DE CHEMINS DE FER VICINAUX*). These 18 cars of the S-type were painted blue with silver stripes in the *FEVE* colour scheme, and put into service on the northern lines while older cars were being refitted. In spite of these improvements ridership started falling during the late 1970s, mainly due to cars becoming available to more and more people. In 1981 totally new cars were ordered for the southern line to VILANOVA DE CASTELLÓ. Ten trains of the 3600-series would be built by Babcock & Wilcox, which helped recuperate many passengers. For the northern lines, 30 units of the UTA 3700-series were ordered from CAF, MACOSA and Brown-Boveri, which began running in 1987. The provision of new trains was not the only strategy to improve service on the 117km long network. There were still 580(!) level crossings, which had to be reduced in order to allow faster and safer operation. More stations were equipped with high platforms to make access into trains easier. However, the most important project was to finally realise the long planned rail link across the city to create an urban modern metro network which is directly connected to the suburban branches served by the five existing lines. Fast and frequent services had to be offered to former villages of Burjassot, Paterna, Alboraia or Torrent which had become dormitory towns of Valencia.

Initially two separate projects were carried out. The first included an underground extension of the BÉTERA and LLÍRIA lines from EMPALME to the Turia river under Pio XII avenue, to serve the densely populated areas at Beniferri and Campanar. The other project was to extend the southern line from its terminus station JESÚS to the *NORTE* railway station, which lies quite close to the city centre, some 200m from the Town Hall. While construction had begun on the JESÚS – *NORTE* section a joint project was approved and a tunnel would be created under Gran Vía de Fernando el Católico and Ramón y Cajal, with two more stations at PLAÇA D'ESPANYA and ÀNGEL GUIMERÀ. The new city tunnel would continue further south along the existing route with JESÚS and HOSPITAL underground stations. The latter would be just under the former stop at Soriano. After that the line would come back to the surface and cross the new Turia river and follow its original alignment to VILANOVA DE CASTELLÓ. Just after the Turia bridge, VALÈNCIA-SUD station would connect to a new depot and workshop. Later even the head office and the metro control centre would be located there.

The 6.7km tunnel was built by the cut-and-cover method with a vaulted roof. At JESÚS, soil had to be frozen to avoid water coming into the construction site. The eight underground stations were spread at an average distance of 800m with 96m long platforms. All of them look quite functional and uniform but, compared to new stations built only ten years later for Line 3, they are too dark and too low. The ceiling is painted black and illumination is limited to the platforms. Along the lower part of the side walls coloured tiles distinguish the eight stations. In 1998, when Line 3 started operating to TORRENT, station panels were also changed in the underground stations. For some years the control centre had its home in the former station building at JESÚS. Started under *FEVE* administration, the new Metro de Valencia, as it would be called from now on, was inaugurated on 8 October 1988 under the new administration of *FERROCARRILS DE LA GENERALITAT VALENCIANA*, a public company depending on the autonomous government of the *Comunitat Valenciana*. The new company, founded in 1986, had taken over all narrow gauge lines in this autonomous region on 1 January 1987. Independent from other lines hundreds of kilometres away, it should be able to solve problems faster and react to needs in a more immediate way than its predecessor whose head office was in Madrid, 300km away.

With the opening of the city tunnel, operation of the existing lines was slightly reorganised and lines were numbered. From then on Line 1 would run from BÉTERA in the north to VILANOVA DE CASTELLÓ in the south (72km with 40 stations). Line 2 would operate between LLÍRIA in the north-west and VALÈNCIA-SUD (and from 1991 as far as TORRENT). The stretch between LLÍRIA and Ademús (which was the name of EMPALME station between 1988 and 1998) is 22.3km, the remaining part of the line is on shared tracks with Line 1 through the city tunnel and further south to TORRENT. On both lines, trains started running every 15 minutes on their double track sections, i.e. SEMINARI – TORRENT and PATERNA – TORRENT thus providing a 7.5 minute headway in the central partly underground section between Ademús (EMPALME) and TORRENT. During peak hours this interval was reduced to 3.5 minutes.

The PONT DE FUSTA – RAFELBUNYOL line (13.4km with 11 stations) would become Line 3 and remain the same for some years still, while the PONT DE FUSTA – El Grao line (from now on Line 4) would be extended to Ademús over the tracks formerly used by the BÉTERA and LLÍRIA trains. This way a new tangential route was created to connect all northern parts of Valencia. Trains on this 9.8km line (14 stops) had to reverse at PONT DE FUSTA to continue their journey.

Lines 3 and 4 were still electrified at 600V (with 3400- and 3500-series trains), whereas the modernised Lines 1 and 2 had 1,500V power supply and were served by new trains of the 3600- and 3700-series ordered from Babcock & Wilcox and from a CAF, MACOSA and Brown-Boveri consortium a few years earlier. While these new trains improved service, the elimination of level crossings in rural areas continued, the overhead wire was completely renewed, new stops were added along the routes and more older stations were fitted with high platforms, which in some cases leaves the original station building on a slightly lower level than the platforms. Ramps or lifts were built at most stations to provide easy access for people with reduced mobility.

On 9 May 1989, PALMARET station (Line 3) opened in the southern part of the Alboraia municipality. This modern surface station would become the northern end of the urban metro service a few years later. On 2 March 1990, at the southern end of Line 1, the section between ALBERIC and VILANOVA DE CASTELLÓ reopened after floods had totally destroyed the line when the Tous reservoir broke in 1982. The terminus station was rebuilt on a better location in that town.

The newly established Line 4 between Ademús and El Grao did not operate for very long. The line had always been a physical barrier for the parts of the city it runs through, and 27 level crossings along the 9.8km route did not really allow an efficient service. Therefore the government decided to close the line down on 31 January 1990 in order to launch a new tramway project, which would integrate a modern means of transport in an urban redevelopment of the area, which was rather degraded then. In its last year the line had carried 3million people. On the day of closure, the Belgian trains (3400-series) were taken out of service. It took two years to start construction of the new line,

Left A 3700-series car in old livery on a northbound service to Paterna at Àngel Guimerà on Line 1.

Right The original station building at Pont de Fusta was the terminus of the northern lines to Bétera, Llíria, Rafelbunyol and El Grao until 1988. Today, tram T4 runs in a loop in front of the building on the square once occupied by several tracks.

Below 3700-series on L-1 service equipped with luggage racks. Capital Transport

which would follow the original alignment. At the former terminus station of Pont de Fusta all tracks (except one for Line 3 which would be maintained until 1995) were dismantled and a large square was created. The new Line 4 (later titled T4) started regular service on 21 May 1994, and was the first modern tramway operating in Spain since the abandonment of the last Spanish system in the 1970s. In the year 2000 it is still the only modern tram line in Spain, although many other cities (like Bilbao, Barcelona, Málaga, Alicante and Sevilla) are beginning construction of modern tramway routes.

Most of T4 runs on separate right-of-way, but unfortunately preference at traffic lights is not always given. The service is provided by 21 low-floor trams built by Siemens-Duewag (3800-series) and all 21 stops have 60m long and 2.5m wide platforms. The line operating between Ademús (now Empalme) and Dr. Lluch is 10.7km long, and provides transfer to Lines 1 and 2 at Ademús and to Line 3 at Pont de Fusta (until 1995) and Benimaclet (since 1995). A loop was built at Pont de Fusta to avoid a change of direction. The eastern end of the line near the beach is also aligned in a 2.1km loop. The tram line provides access to the large University campus in the north of Valencia.

The next step to create a real metro network for Valencia was the construction of Lines 3 and 5 within the city itself. Line 3 should run through a new tunnel from PALMARET to ALAMEDA where it would join Line 5, a new east-west axis running totally underground between Cabanyal and Mislata. This line would be excavated by tunnelling machines in order to avoid disruption of traffic and commercial activity on the surface. Trains would run in single track tube tunnels and there would be 12 stations along the route: Cabanyal (transfer to *RENFE*), Blasco Ibáñez, República Argentina, Aragón, ALAMEDA, COLÓN, XÀTIVA, ÀNGEL GUIMERÀ, Avinguda (now AV. DEL CID), NOU D'OCTUBRE, MISLATA and Nuevo Cauce (now MISLATA-ALMASSIL).

In 1992, construction began on Line 3 using the *cut-and-cover* method for the 3km tunnel, which included four underground stations at an average distance of 600m: ALAMEDA, FACULTATS, BENIMACLET and MACHADO. Just before PALMARET the line returns to the surface and continues on the original Line 3 tracks to RAFELBUNYOL (which was changed to 1,500V). Along the surface section platforms had to be lengthened to a minimum of 60m and ramps for easy access were built.

The tunnel lies only 10m deep and thus access to stations is quick and easy. Compared to the underground stations on the first city tunnel, stations along the new route are more spacious and include some artistic elements, with murals and sculptures in vestibules and platform areas. Unfortunately illumination is not sufficient to show these pieces of art properly. Alameda station was designed by Valencia's outstanding architect Santiago Calatrava, and lies under the former Turia river bed. This station was built together with a new bridge on top by the same architect. As a future junction for Lines 3 and 5 it was built with four tracks and two side and one central platform. Near Machado station a new depot and workshop were built for this line.

The new underground section opened for traffic on 5 May 1995 and introduced a new type of rolling stock for the Metro de Valencia. 18 trains of the 3900-series had been built by GEC Alsthom in Albuixec near Valencia. The 45m long trains consist of two motor cars and a trailer in the middle and are of the modern walk-through type. Frequency of trains was 7.5 minutes on the underground section between ALAMEDA and PALMARET and 15 minutes on the surface section to RAFELBUNYOL. At BENIMACLET easy transfer is provided to T4, with the tram stop directly on top of the metro station.

During 1996, Les Carolines station on former Line 2 (now Line 1) was renamed LES CAROLINES / FIRA (Fairgrounds), as this station is closer to the exhibition centre than BENIMÀMET, which had carried this suffix until then (since summer 1999, the Fairgrounds can also be reached by T4). By the end of the year the surface section of Line 3 had been totally equipped for ATP operation. The following year an automatic brake system (*Frenado Automático Puntual*) was installed along Lines 1 and 2 (now Line 1) which acts similarly to the ATP control system, and stops the train in case the

Left Two 3-car trains meeting at ALAMEDA, the left one runs to RAFELBUNYOL and the right one into the city centre. On the left, tracks are ready for the future Line 5. This huge station, designed by Santiago Calatrava, lies directly under the old riverbed park with exits on either bank of the former river Turia.

Right AVINGUDA DEL CID is one of the most impressive stations along the western extension of Line 3. The central track, seen in the foreground, is not used during normal operation.

driver doesn't react to certain signals or reduces speed at certain points along the line. During 2000, along Line 1 a series of accidents were reported by the local press, caused by failure of barriers at a number of level crossings on the outer branches. For some months this situation led to strikes by train drivers.

Meanwhile construction on Line 5 had begun on the central section through the city centre. While the running tunnels were built by a tunnelling machine (which would later excavate Madrid's L8 MAR DE CRISTAL – CAMPO DE LAS NACIONES section), stations were excavated by the cut-and-cover method. This method was also used to create a connection between the new tunnel and JESÚS station on the first city tunnel, using part of the tunnel excavated some ten years earlier between JESÚS and the *NORTE* Railway station. No station was included on this connecting tunnel, although there is an option to add one later within the plans of rebuilding Valencia's main railway station (underground and with a cross-city tunnel north to allow through train service).

When the new line finally opened on 16 September 1998 after some delay due to water infiltration at XÀTIVA station, it was connected to the existing Line 3 instead of creating a separate Line 5. This way a direct link could be offered between RAFELBUNYOL and AVINGUDA DEL CID (formerly called Avinguda) and JESÚS with trains running through to TORRENT. The inaugurated stretch was 3.2km long between ALAMEDA and AVINGUDA DEL CID, with an approximately 1km long branch to JESÚS and has four stations in the heart of the city. COLÓN lies in the centre of the shopping district and can be accessed by two double sets of escalators. Passenger flow upwards and downwards is totally separated here. The main entrance is on a square where the foundations of a former city gate, the Gate of the Jews, were uncovered. XÀTIVA is close to the Town Hall and just outside the fantastic early 20th century building of Estació del Nord (main railway terminus). In this station, both platforms lie on top of each other, with westbound tracks on the lower level. This way trains coming from COLÓN can turn off towards JESÚS without crossing tracks. The junction is situated just before arriving at XÀTIVA, so southbound trains are visible from the westbound platform. ÀNGEL GUIMERÀ serves the western side of the old town and provides quite easy transfer to Lines 1 and 2 which, from the day of inauguration of the Line 3 extension, would become Line 1 (with two northern branches).

The central location of these new stations put expectations high for rising ridership, and passen-

gers did not stay away. With only 3.5 months of operation of the Line 3 extension, overall ridership on the Metro de Valencia rose by almost 15 per cent in 1998. COLÓN became the busiest station on the network, and stations along the ALAMEDA – RAFELBUNYOL section also increased traffic substantially as they were now within easy reach of many parts of the city. FACULTATS (which serves the University) even surpassed COLÓN on certain days.

After trains started operating between ALAMEDA and JESÚS and further on to TORRENT, the service on Line 1 was reduced on outer branches from a basic 30-minute interval to 45 minutes, and so-called *semidirectos* were introduced, i.e. trains skipping some stations to reduce travel times. Following a passengers' protest a more frequent timetable was introduced on most sections.

In 1998, *Ferrocarrils de la Generalitat* changed the corporate image of the metro. Instead of the company's yellow 'V' on white background, the new logo shows a white 'm' inside a red circle. The network is simply named *METRO VALENCIA* which, like *METROBILBAO* makes it sound more modern than the classical *METRO DE VALENCIA*. Since then many trains running on Line 1 have been repainted in the new red and white colour scheme.

On 3 March 1999, shortly before a further underground section opened, tram line T4 was extended westwards from EMPALME to TVV (*Televisió Valenciana*) (2.3km). Four new trams, air-conditioned like those of the first series, were bought to cover the new stretch. In summer 1999, T4 trams reached the Valencia Fairgrounds (*Fira de València*) (0.8km).

On 20 May 1999, the western section of Line 3 (2.4km) was added to the successful network with three new underground stations: NOU D'OCTUBRE, MISLATA and MISLATA-ALMASSIL (formerly planned as Nuevo Cauce). This section, both tunnels and stations, had been built by the *cut-and-cover* method and serves more than 50,000 people in the town of Mislata. These three stations, all with side platforms, are quite similar in design – side walls are covered with tiles, basically white with colour elements giving a feeling of spaciousness. Like all the other stations built in the 1990s, these are also equipped with elevators. This section follows a former railway alignment of the *SOCIEDAD DE LOS FERROCARRILES DE VALENCIA Y ARAGÓN* which operated a line as far as Llíria from 1889 until 1968 when the line, now terminating at Riba-roja, was redirected along the new river Turia to enter the central station from the south. In the future the metro might continue westwards along this route.

A L–3 train waiting to leave for a Palmaret service (every 15 minutes) on a side track at Torrent. The two tracks on the right merge just south of the station and run as a regional line, with request stops, to Villanueva de Castellón.

In September 1999, 12 months after the opening of the Alameda – Avinguda del Cid section, *Metro Valencia* had reached 33million passengers a year. Compared to 21million in 1997 and 24.2million in 1998 this represents a spectacular increase. Of all stations, Colón became the busiest, with 2.4million passengers entering this station in one year, followed by Xàtiva with 1.9million. Also all other stations in the city centre have greatly improved passenger figures.

With this extension, this phase of the metro expansion project was finished. Original plans to build Line 5 east to Cabanyal had been reconsidered for some years and finally a different solution was decided upon. Instead of building a full metro line, a light metro would be built to reduce costs. This would be similar to a *Stadtbahn* network operating in many German cities (Stuttgart, Hannover, Cologne, Bonn, Frankfurt, etc.) or the *Premetro* or *Sneltram* in Belgium or the Netherlands (Antwerp, Charleroi, Brussels, Amsterdam, Rotterdam, etc.). Trains will run through the Line 3 tunnel between Alameda and Mislata-Almassil, but continue on the surface in other areas. After long discussions during 1998 and 1999 a compromise was found: Line 5 will continue underground towards the east from Alameda as far as Parque Ayora with two more underground stations in between. After the Alameda junction the line will follow its originally planned alignment towards Aragón (near the Mestalla stadium). Then, instead of turning into Yecla and Blasco Ibáñez streets, it will continue straight under Santos Justos y Pastor street, where the second station will be located at the crossroads with Dr. Manuel Candela street, and the last underground station right under the Ayora gardens. Construction contracts for this underground section to be built by *cut-and-over* were awarded in September 2000 to NECSO-Torrescámara-Dragados and service is scheduled to start in 2002. After Parque Ayora trains will bear southwards and will come to the surface in Jerónimo Monsoriu street, where the first street level stop will be. Along Francisco Cubells street they will reach the harbour area (also referred to as Balcón al Mar) at Plaza Armada Española, where they will turn northwards to meet tram line T4 at Mediterráneo street. A branch will continue straight on from Plaza Armada Española towards Neptuno Avenue near the Arenas beach. These surface stations will be located in green areas to reduce their visual impact on the environment. The whole new eastern extension will be 4.7km long, of which 2.5km will be in tunnel. The surface section might open for regular service in 2003. At the western end of Line 3, a short tunnel was added to allow the future crossing of the new Turia river in a false tunnel. Line 5 trains would then continue along today's *Renfe* alignment towards Manises Airport (2004), and further west to Riba-roja (2006). Once finished, the new Line 5 will have three very different sections, the western part

NOU D'OCTUBRE – large *cut-and-cover* stations are a common feature along the western branch of Line 3. Side walls are covered with white tiles and colour images.

being like a suburban rail service with maximum speeds of up to 100km/h, the central part will operate as a full metro (together with Line 3) and the eastern part will be a modern light rail or tram link. For this purpose, new trains were ordered which can adapt themselves to the different voltage used along these three different sections.

Another mid-term project for Valencia is a second light rail line, similar to Line 5. This line, shown as T2, will be a north-south link and run partly underground in the city centre between Parc Central (new railway station) and Almazora street, north of PONT DE FUSTA. Starting in Orriols in the north of the city, it will run under the old town to XÀTIVA (Line 3 and current central railway station), and then continue southeast to provide a transit link for the 'Arts & Science City', now under con-

MISLATA-ALMASSIL is the current western terminus of the line, which will be extended to the airport above ground. The tree shaped images on the walls seem to remind us of the rural landscape on top of the station, now densely populated.

struction, and the neighbourhood of Natzaret on the southern side of the port. The alignment of the central section depends on a *Renfe* decision to build a cross-city mainline tunnel. Both links could also be constructed together. In the northern part of Valencia, people asked for a station adjacent to the metro depot situated on the surface west of Machado station on L–3.

In order to improve transfer facilities at Empalme (L–1 and T4), in 2000 this station was rebuilt 150m south of its original location in 2000. Both lines now share the same platform and elevators make access easier for everybody. This new solution also avoids the huge gap formerly existing between the platform and trains coming in from Bétera as this platform was in a curve. Campanar, Túria and San Isidre will be equipped with elevators.

In Torrent an extension will be built to improve access to the centre of this town. While Line 1 turns southwards towards Villanueva de Castellón after Torrent station, a branch would continue westwards and a new station would be added to the network on Avenida País Valencià.

Above Elegant modern station entrances were built along the western Line 3 (this one at Mislata-Almassil). The whole line is fully accessible. Here the elevator can be seen on the right.

Left Original Art Nouveau ticket windows inside Valencia's main railway station. In 2000, tariff integration did not yet include *Renfe* trains.

OPERATION AND FARE SYSTEM

On weekdays the Valencia Metro operates from 05:00 to 24:00 at these frequencies:

Line 1:

On central section (Empalme – Torrent) … … every 7.5 minutes
On double track sections
(Empalme – Paterna, Empalme – Seminari) … every 15 minutes
On single track sections
(Paterna – Llíria, Seminari – Bétera,
Torrent – Villanueva de Castellón) … … every 30–45 minutes

Line 3:

On urban section (Mislata-Almassil – Palmaret) every 7.5 minutes
On surface section (Palmaret – Rafelbunyol) … every 15 minutes
On L1/L3 route (Torrent – Palmaret) … … every 15 minutes

These basic frequencies are reduced at weekends and slightly increased during rush hours. Trains run on a fixed timetable which is posted in all stations.

Tickets

In November 1996, the first integrated tickets for both metro and EMT city buses for use within Valencia city were introduced. In February 2000 tariff integration was greatly improved by including suburban buses and the entire metro system into one fare system (called *Metrobús*). Negotiations to expand this fare system to the *Renfe Cercanías* service (as in Madrid) might conclude soon. The covered area, which serves some 1.4 million people, is divided into three ring zones: A; B; C; of which Zone A basically matches the municipalities of Valencia and Mislata (formerly referred to as Zone AV). This new fare system significantly reduces prices for the average user, so it might help to

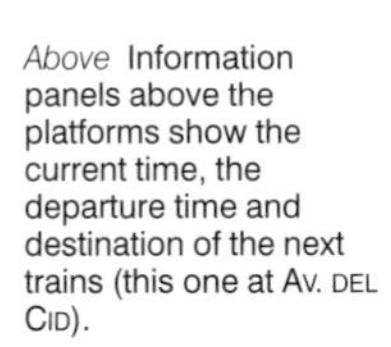

Above Information panels above the platforms show the current time, the departure time and destination of the next trains (this one at Av. del Cid).

Right The almost oversized Alameda station designed by Santiago Calatrava will be the future junction for lines 3 and 5 and was therefore built with four tracks.

increase overall usage of public transport in the Valencia metropolitan area, which is considered to be among the lowest in comparison with similar European cities. A ticket for a single journey is now €0.78 for one zone, €1.05 for two zones and €1.77 for three. A Bono Metro (10 trips) is €4.35 for one zone, €6.17 for two zones and €8.80 for three zones. Unfortunately there are no maps available which include all means of transport; the 2000 edition of EMT's bus map does not even show metro stops opened in 1998!

Tickets have to be introduced into validating machines when entering and when leaving the underground stations, although access to surface stations is without barriers. Along rural sections ticket collectors still punch your ticket manually.

Passenger numbers have been increasing year after year since the Valencia Metro was launched in 1988. Between 1993 and 1999 journeys increased from 17.7 million to 28.6 million. Since Line 3 Alameda – Mislata-Almassil opened, the line doubled its ridership from 6.8 to 13.6 million by 31 October 1999. These figures are encouraging, although they are still quite low compared, for example, with Bilbao where Line 1 is only 24km long but carries 50million passengers a year. As described in the introductory chapter, the urban Valencia Metro is now similar in length but has an additional 90km of suburban/rural feeder lines.

A repainted 3700-series train is leaving Empalme for Bétera. A new station 150m further south will improve transfer between lines.

A 3700-series car of the 2nd series has left Empalme for Bétera. These carriages can be easily distinguished from the 1st series by their different front.

Valencia

Inside a 3900-series car in service on Line 3. So far, only 3-car trains of the walk-through type have been used, but a fourth carriage was ordered in 2000 to increase capacity on the line. Stations are announced acoustically and an arrow above the doors indicates the side of the station's platform. A dot matrix above the doors shows the internal temperature.

VALENCIA METRO – ROLLING STOCK

Metro Line	**1**	**1**	**1**	**3**	**T4**
Year:	1981	1987	1990	1995	1994/1999
Series No.		3700	3700	3900	
Type	Babcock Wilcox	UTA 1st series	UTA 2nd series	UTE	TRAMVIA unidirectional
Units in operation	10	30	10	18	21+4
Cars per unit	3	2	2	3	3
Produced by	Babcock Wilcox	CAF	CAF	GEC Alsthom	Siemens
Electrical equipment	GEE	BBC	BBC	GEC Alsthom	Siemens
Tension	1500V	1500V	1500V	1500V	750V
Capacity: seated	83	102	102	92	65
standing	350	138	138	342	136
Length: metres	47.16	30	30	45	23.78
Width: metres	2.55	2.55	2.55	2.55	2.4
Power per unit: KW	486	376	376	1312	432
Power supply	DC	Chopper DC	Chopper DC	AC	AC
Max. speed: km/h	80	80	80	80	65
Acceleration: m/sec	0.8	1	1	1.1	1.1
Weight: tonne	74.6	44	46	96	30

All trains use a pantograph for power collection and have 1000mm gauge. 3900-series trains are equipped with ATP and are ready for ATO. In 2000, trailers were ordered to form 4-car trains along Line 3 and thus increase capacities.

BILBAO METRO

Right Moyua – unfortunately no escalators were installed between platforms and vestibule in the new underground stations, although full accessibility is provided by lifts situated at the end of the platforms.

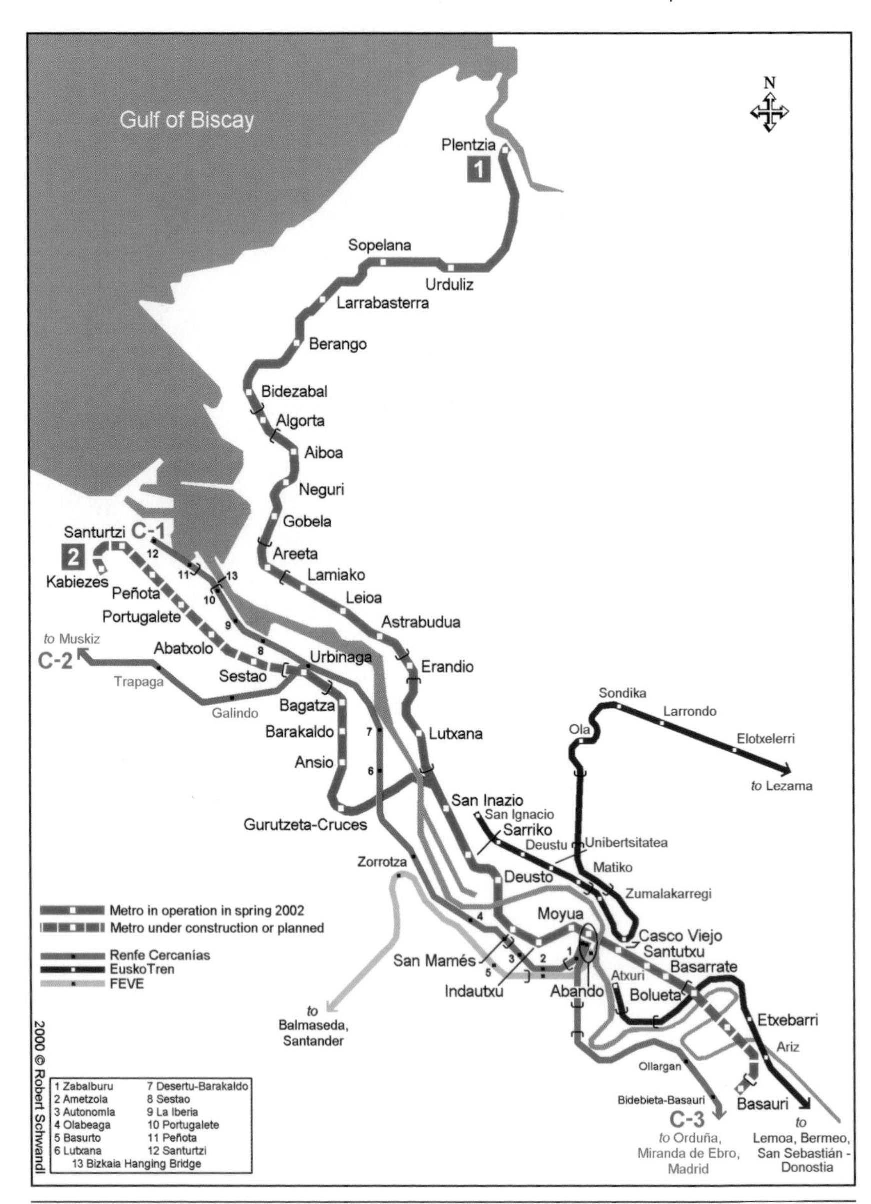

INTRODUCTION

Bilbao (Bilbo in Basque) lies 400km north of Madrid and 620km northwest of Barcelona. The city is the capital of the province of Bizkaia (Vizcaya), one of the three provinces that constitute the autonomous region of Euskadi (País Vasco - Basque Country) which, like Catalonia or Valencia, is officially bilingual, Spanish and Basque. Although the municipality of Bilbao has only 370,000 inhabitants it is the centre of a metropolitan area with around 1 million people. Bilbao lies some 15km from the sea (Gulf of Biscay) and is the most important industrial centre and harbour in northern Spain. The metropolitan area spreads out along both sides of the river Nervión, also called Ría de Bilbao as it is navigable as far as Bilbao. Along the left bank the industrial towns of Barakaldo, Sestao, Portugalete and Santurtzi contain some 300,000 inhabitants, whereas 120,000 people live on the more residential right bank. 100,000 more populate the Ibaizabal valley southeast of Bilbao (Etxebarri, Basauri), and some 50,000 spread out along the Asua valley around Lezama and the Sondika airport. The official use of both languages is not as regulated as in Catalonia, therefore Spanish and Basque names are often used indiscriminately, especially as far as spelling is concerned. So the visitor may read Santurtzi (Basque) or Santurce (Spanish), Lutxana / Luchana, San Inazio / San Ignacio or Areeta / Las Arenas. This book uses the names and spellings used by the different rail operators in their publications or on their maps.

Due to its industrial tradition, Bilbao also has had a long association with rail transport. For over a century the city had no less than six terminal stations in central Bilbao. Two had Spanish standard gauge (1672mm): Abando was served by the dominant *Norte* Rail Company, and linked Bilbao to Madrid and Barcelona via Miranda de Ebro (opened in 1863); La Naja was the terminal for the Bilbao – Santurtzi line. This station situated next to Arenal Bridge under the *FEVE* Bilbao terminal was closed in 1999 after the *Renfe Cercanías* trains were redirected via the southern route to Abando. The other four terminal stations were served by 1000mm narrow gauge lines, most of them built in the 19th century to connect the mines around the city and along the northern coast to industrial sites and the harbour near Bilbao. Atxuri is still the terminus for *EuskoTren* trains to Gernika, Bermeo and Donostia/San Sebastián; Concordia (next to Abando) is still the *FEVE* terminus for trains to Balmaseda, Santander and Oviedo along the northern coast; Calzadas (next to

Plaza Unamuno) used to be the terminus for trains from Lezama; and San Nicolás was the terminus for trains to Plentzia. The latter two were connected in 1996, Calzadas was abandoned and San Nicolás is now Casco Viejo / Zazpi Kaleak on the *EuskoTren* San Ignacio – Lezama service.

A trip on Line 1 of the Bilbao Metro takes the passenger through some very different parts of the metropolitan area. The line starts at Bolueta in southeastern Bilbao on an elevated structure built on top of the *EuskoTren* line to Gernika, Bermeo and Donostia / San Sebastián, for which a new station was also built to provide comfortable transfer between both networks. Immediately after leaving the station the metro enters the cross-city tunnel running through several very similar stations which like all the surface stations are fully wheel chair accessible (Basarrate – Deusto). After serving the very densely populated areas around Basarrate and Santutxu, the metro reaches Casco Viejo (old town centre), one of the busiest stations along the line, due to its transfer facility to the *EuskoTren* line to Lezama and to San Ignacio along the right side of the river. One exit of this station is via a lift (opened in 1996 and 50m high), which takes you up to the Mallona park and the Begoña district, from where you can enjoy a great view over the city. Between Casco Viejo and Abando, the River Nervión is crossed underground for the first time (see History section to learn more about construction of this section). Abando station is located under Plaza Circular and is directly connected to Bilbao's main railway station, which in the future should become a large intermodal station for all public transport in and around the city. This metro station serves the central shopping district along Gran Vía Don Diego López de Haro (named after the founder of Bilbao). The metro continues under this central artery and arrives at Plaza Moyua (also referred to as Plaza Elíptica due to its oval shape), which is the heart of the Ensanche, the modern part of central Bilbao, a few minutes away from the Guggenheim Museum.

After Moyua the metro takes a light turn to the left, and under Ercilla street it reaches the next station Indautxu which was built under an existing underground shopping gallery. After turning right again to continue parallel to its former alignment trains arrive at the next station, San Mamés, which is situated next to the football stadium of the same name, home to the Athletic de Bilbao football club, and very near the Exhibition Centre and the central bus station. In 1999, *Renfe Cercanías* established a new station at San Mamés, thus creating one of the big transfer hubs within Bilbao.

After San Mamés the line takes a 90 degree turn to the right and crosses under the River Nervión

Left *FEVE's* Bilbao terminus Concordia station lies almost on top of *Renfe's* former La Naja terminus next to Arenal bridge. Bilbao's main railway station Abando would be some 50m behind it.

Right Moyua is a typical Foster station along the underground section through the city centre. The whole platform area can be overlooked from the entrance barrier concourse.

for the second time, before it reaches Deusto on the right bank of the river. This is one of the areas that take most advantage of the metro, as connections between Deusto and the Moyua / Abando areas were strongly improved. Deusto, situated under Iruña street, is among the busiest stations on the line.

A sharp turn left aligns the metro parallel to the river for several kilometres. The next two stations, Sarriko and San Inazio, were built by the cut-and-cover method and therefore have a different shape. Instead of the typical cavern seen in the other underground stations, these two are rectangular. Sarriko is very high with a huge glass entrance structure that allows daylight to come in. San Inazio was designed as the junction for lines 1 and 2, and therefore has three tracks with one central (for Bolueta bound trains) and one side platform (for outbound trains).

San Inazio is one of the few cut-and-cover stations of the network, and at the junction between the two metro lines it has three tracks, two for incoming trains with a central platform, and the one seen in the background for outbound trains.

After SAN INAZIO the metro line divides into two branches. Line 1 comes up to the surface and continues along the right bank of the Nervión to Getxo and PLENTZIA (using the existing rail line), whereas Line 2 remains underground until shortly before arriving at its temporary terminus station at URBINAGA.

The first surface station on Line 1 is LUTXANA (in the municipality of Erandio), from where a branch turns off right towards Sondika, which is under *EUSKOTREN* responsibility, but not at present in service, but is included in a light rail project for the Asua-Valley. As long as no transfer is possible here, LUTXANA station will remain one of the least frequented ones on the network.

The next station, ERANDIO, was put underground in 1988 before construction of the metro started. This is why it originally had a different design to the other underground stations, but in 1998 it was refurbished and walls were covered to integrate it better with the overall design of the metro.

After ERANDIO the line continues on the surface close to the river, with views over industrial estates on both sides of the river, reminders of Bilbao's glorious past as a centre of heavy steel industry. After passing some shipyards we arrive at ASTRABUDUA, which is a surface station and used to be known as Axpe-Udondo. The line passes more industrial sites to LEIOA station, used mainly by students transferring to the bus shuttle for the Campus of the University of the Basque Country. A light rail line is planned to cover this diverse municipality and the university in the future.

LAMIAKO (still in the Leioa municipality) is among the least frequented stations of the line, with some schools and companies in its neighbourhood. After this station the metro enters the municipality of Getxo, which spreads out along the mouth of the River Nervión and which is the most densely populated municipality on the right bank. The first station AREETA (formerly Las Arenas) was built underground, as it is located in the centre of the Getxo shopping district. This station is the busiest outside Bilbao city. It is also within walking distance of the Hanging Bridge between Areeta and Portugalete on the left bank of the river (see 'Other Rail Transport in Bilbao'). Just after AREETA station the metro line turns right and returns to the surface. For the next few kilometres it winds through pleasant residential areas. The next stop, GOBELA, which opened a few months after the other stations in June 1996, is an elevated station with a central platform. After NEGURI and AIBOA, both at grade, trains reach the last of the new underground stations, ALGORTA.

BIDEZABAL station was built to replace the former stop some 300m further north called Getxo. It gets very busy during the summer with people going to the nearby beach of Arrigunaga. People in the neighbourhood are now asking for the reconstruction of the former Getxo station and the line in this area to be put underground, which would enable the elimination of the last level crossing.

After BIDEZABAL the metro leaves the built-up area of Getxo and the surroundings become more and more rural. As a result of the new metro service the following towns of BERANGO and LARRABASTERRA are growing steadily. The latter is the final stop for some trains and therefore its station has three tracks.

After SOPELANA station, a depot and workshop were built for the new metro trains. URDULIZ marks the end of the double-track route, and from here trains descend to sea level in a steep gradient (21 per cent) with tight curves and two short tunnels (18m and 41m long). Along this very rural stretch you might spot some cows grazing beside the line, which is now totally protected on both sides.

After three kilometres the train reaches its final station at PLENTZIA, a seaside town connected to the station via a new footbridge. The terminal station of Line 1 is equipped with four tracks. A trip from BOLUETA to PLENTZIA takes 45 minutes.

Left A metro train heading for PLENTZIA is leaving AREETA underground station in Getxo, a pleasant residential area close to the sea.

Right The last stretch of metro Line 1 between URDULIZ and PLENTZIA is single track and runs through woods and meadows. A 20-minute headway is operated along this rural section.

Line 2 turns off the common trunk line just after leaving SAN INAZIO station. Trains turn left and dive deeper to cross the river Nervión for the third time. After almost 3km they arrive at the first station within the Barakaldo municipality, GURUTZETA / CRUCES, which serves a large residential area and a huge hospital complex. The second station, ANSIO is in the middle of an important industrial area with heavy steel industry, which is now being redeveloped. BARAKALDO station lies in the heart of the municipality between Plaza Bide Onera/Fueros Ave and Elcano Street. The next station, BAGATZA (between Santa Teresa Sq. and Gabriel Aresti St.) serves the northern part of this populous town.

Barakaldo is separated from its neighbouring town of Sestao by the wide valley of the River Galindo. Therefore the metro crosses the river on a viaduct and meets the *RENFE CERCANÍAS* lines to SANTURTZI and MUSKIZ at the new elevated transfer station URBINAGA. For a couple of years, until the next stretch to SESTAO is finished, URBINAGA is the end of Line 2 (5.9km).

After URBINAGA (situated in the municipality of Sestao), Line 2 will go back into a tunnel for the rest of its route. It will run parallel to the river, but further uphill than the existing *RENFE* line, which runs close to the river. This way the metro will be nearer to the town centres of SESTAO (one station of the same name), Portugalete (three stations, ABATXOLO, PORTUGALETE, PEÑOTA) and Santurtzi (two stations, SANTURTZI, KABIEZES). The time schedule published in spring 2000 plans to reach SESTAO in 2004, PORTUGALETE in 2006, SANTURTZI in 2008 and KABIEZES in 2012.

Both lines will be extended 3km south from BOLUETA to BASAURI with one intermediate station at ETXEBARRI. Although initially planned to be carried out after finishing Line 2 along the right bank, the elevated extension to ETXEBARRI might be built earlier (2004) as it does not include any tunnelling, but the construction of a second depot necessary for the new trains running on Line 2. Between BOLUETA and ETXEBARRI the metro will follow the former alignment of the Matiko – Ariz-Azbarren narrow gauge line which is still visible although it has been out of service for more than 30 years. The increase of traffic along the trunk line with the opening of the first section of Line 2 made it necessary to extend the original line 500m south from BOLUETA towards ETXEBARRI, in order to allow a more flexible changing of tracks. Between ETXEBARRI and BASAURI another station could be added at Ariz.

Eventually all trains will terminate in the underground station of BASAURI in 2012. The total length of the network will then be 42km:

L1 + L2:	BASAURI – SAN INAZIO	...	10km
L1:	SAN INAZIO – PLENTZIA	...	21km
L2:	SAN INAZIO – KABIEZES	...	11km

HISTORY OF THE METRO

The first proposal for a metropolitan railway in Bilbao dates back to 1924, just after Madrid and Barcelona had inaugurated the first metro lines in Spain. The proposed line should have run from Atxuri to Basurto via Abando.

In the 1930s it became obvious that the large number of existing terminal stations was not really helpful for passengers, so a plan to unite all different lines in one terminal building at Abando, where the Norte railway company had its terminal, was presented. The Spanish Civil War interrupted this project which was eventually rediscovered in the 1990s and is now slowly being realised.

Like most big cities in Spain, Bilbao and its metropolitan area had also grown strongly during the decades of the 1950s and 1960s, so a solution to the increasing traffic problems had to be found. In 1971 the *Comisión de Comunicaciones de Vizcaya* was founded to co-ordinate transport within the province of Bizkaia, of which Bilbao is the capital.

During the following years several alternatives were discussed for a metropolitan railway in Bilbao and its adjacent municipalities along the River Nervión. The first alternative included a Y-shaped system which should start at Basauri southeast of Bilbao, run through central Bilbao, and then split into two branches at San Inazio towards Santurtzi and Getxo on either side of the river. The junction could also be built near the San Mamés stadium, which would reduce the river crossings and also serve left-bank areas like Olabeaga and Zorrotza. For the stretch along the right-bank to Getxo an existing rail alignment could be used. This first alternative proposed a second line which would run underground from Rekaldeberri to Otxarkoaga and cross the first line, in a right angle at Plaza Moyua in the heart of modern Bilbao.

The second alternative was based on the first but included a common trunk line as far as Sestao on the left bank where the line would split, towards Santurtzi and Plentzia (crossing the river towards Areeta). The section between San Inazio and Areeta could also be included.

The third alternative was similar to the others, but would also include the existing line to Lezama which would be extended into the city as far as Moyua, which would function as a central hub.

In those days the general characteristics of the future metro network were defined: 200m minimum radius, 35 per cent maximum gradient, 80km/h max. speed, standard European gauge, 1,500Vdc and 115m platforms for 5-car trains.

The current terminus at BOLUETA was built on the surface and on top of a new *EUSKOTREN* station on the San Sebastián line. From here the metro will continue south across the river Nervión to Basauri in a few years.

San Mamés station – concrete, glass and stainless steel were the only materials used in underground stations, which can only be distinguished by their names.

In 1975 the newly founded *Consorcio de Transportes de Vizcaya* became responsible for metro studies and two years later, in 1977, a construction plan was approved. Unfortunately the arrival of democracy stopped the whole process, as no major decisions were taken until the new institutions were fully functioning. Like Catalonia, the Basque Country gained its autonomy and the new autonomous government immediately carried out transport studies for the Bilbao metropolitan area, and awarded contracts for construction projects in 1984. Eventually in 1987 the section Casco Viejo – San Inazio – Plentzia, as proposed in the 1970s was approved, which included the suburban line between Lutxana and Plentzia, then operated by Basque Railways (*Eusko Trenbideak*). As this line used 1000mm gauge, the final decision for the metro was also in favour of this gauge, although the branch to Santurtzi should still be built with 1435mm gauge adding a third rail along the common underground stretch in central Bilbao between San Inazio and Basauri. A new company called *IMEBISA* (*Ingeñería del Metro de Bilbao, S.A.*) was set up, which is responsible for planning and co-ordinating construction work, and which depends directly on the *Consorcio de Transportes de Vizcaya*.

Before construction really began on the new section in central Bilbao, Erandio station on the Plentzia line was placed underground in 1988, in the course of a major redevelopment project in the Erandio town centre. Construction of the new underground route under the centre of Bilbao started in 1989.

In 1993 *Metro Bilbao, S.A.* was founded, a company owned entirely by the *Consorcio de Transportes de Vizcaya*. On 1 November 1995 *EuskoTren* (Basque Railways) stopped operating along the Plentzia line, which was handed over to *Metro Bilbao* on 10 November 1995. On 11 November 1995 the new trains started operating along the first stretch between Casco Viejo and Plentzia, introducing the fourth metro system in Spain. On the first weekend, travel was free, and thousands came to explore their new metro. On Plaza Moyua an exhibition showed locomotives and carriages which were in use years ago on narrow gauge lines around Bilbao.

As in Valencia, the metro was converted from a long existing rail line into a modern urban means of transport, which has become extremely successful. The history of the incorporated line goes back to the 19th century. In 1887 a private company built a narrow gauge line from Bilbao to Las Arenas (now Areeta). The line had its Bilbao terminal at San Agustín next to the Town Hall. In 1893 another company built another narrow gauge line from Las Arenas to the seaside resort of Plencia. Both companies were soon taken over by the major narrow gauge rail company operating along the

Left A bird's-eye view of *EuskoTren* Casco Viejo/Zazpi Kaleak station seen from the open-air Begoña elevator. The tunnel entrance behind the peculiar stairs leads to the loop towards the line to Lezama, which used to have its terminus Calzadas only a short distance away. The new metro station lies below and under the mountain to the left.

Right A modern platform roof was built adjacent to the original station building at the Plentzia terminus.

northern Spanish coast, the *Compañía de los Ferrocarriles de Bilbao a Santander*, which strongly invested in the Plentzia line. A short tunnel was built from San Agustín to San Nicolás (now Casco Viejo) to take the Bilbao terminus closer to the city centre, the line was double tracked as far as Algorta by 1926, and totally electrified by 1929. In 1918 a branch was built from Matiko to Ariz-Azbarren to establish a link to the other lines operated by this company. Due to the history of the Plentzia line, until 1957 Las Arenas was a terminal station and trains continuing to Plentzia had to change direction there.

In 1947, the Bilbao – Plentzia Line was handed over to the new transport operator called *Ferrocarriles y Transportes Suburbanos* (*FTS*), which was founded in order to improve the overall transport service in the entire metropolitan area, and which also included the narrow gauge lines from Bilbao to Lezama and from Lutxana to Mungia, with transfer facilities between the three lines at Lutxana and Sondika. The other two lines were also electrified, and the double track section along the Plentzia Line was extended to Larrabasterra with a new station at Las Arenas, to avoid the reversing of trains.

Like most private railway companies in Spain, in those days also the *FTS* got into financial problems during the 1960s and struggled to survive. In 1969 an earth slide badly damaged the Matiko – Ariz-Azbarren branch, and the section between Bilbao-Calzadas and Ciudad Jardín on the Lezama Line. The first was closed down whereas the latter remained without service for some time. In 1975 another section, Sondika – Mungia, had to be closed due to the expansion of Bilbao Airport at Sondika. As the company did not recover from its financial problems, in 1977 the network was provisionally handed over to the state owned *FEVE*, and one year later, in 1978, the newly founded company *Eusko Trenbideak / Ferrocarriles Vascos* (Basque Railways depending on the new autonomous Basque government) took charge of the narrow gauge network in the Basque Country.

After the main section of the Plentzia Line was incorporated into the new metro line a short tunnel was built under Ascao street in the old part of Bilbao between San Nicolás (terminus for the Plentzia Line) and Calzadas (terminus for the Lezama Line) to allow through traffic on both branches, still operated as a loop in 2000 by *EuskoTren* between San Ignacio and Lezama via the new station called Casco Viejo / Zazpi Kaleak (opened in 1996), which provides easy transfer to the metro.

The initial section of the modern metro was 20.5km long and had 24 stations. A section of 6.3km between Casco Viejo and San Inazio is newly built and crosses the heart of Bilbao underground. Next to Arenal bridge, between Casco Viejo and Abando, a new building houses the head

office of *Metro Bilbao,* where the metro control centre is located. Between Sopelana and Urduliz a large depot and workshop was built.

In Bilbao the new metro was not an isolated project, but part of an overall revitalisation programme of a formerly heavily industrialised city. The traditional steel industry had been in crisis for a long time and had to be either modernised or closed down. In central Bilbao a large area along the river Nervión was torn down to be redeveloped. The outstanding, and already world-famous Guggenheim Museum, was inaugurated there in 1997, and nearby the Euskalduna Congress Centre and Music Hall followed soon after. The city wanted to take advantage of the spirit of renewal and build a metro which was not only functional, but also representative for the new era. Renowned architects were invited to design something special for the metro. Among them was *'Architekturengruppe U-Bahn'* who had designed Vienna's and Vancouver's metro system, and Santiago Calatrava, who is the author of the outstanding Alameda metro station in Valencia and the Oriente Railway Station in Lisbon, but eventually the British architect Norman Foster was chosen to give the metro this special touch and to make it one of the new landmarks of the city. His project was given the go ahead because it suggested a clear perception of underground spaces, which definitely increases the feeling of safety and protection by means of simplicity in harmony with end-of-the-millennium minimalist aesthetics. The clear lines of his design would be visible from the surface in the form of the popularly known 'Fosteritos', throughout the access corridors and within the spacious caverns of the stations, which should not be perceived as claustrophobic or stifling. After entering the metro through one of the glass covered accesses (fosteritos) the passenger goes down to the distribution level and the platform in a logical direction, without winding corridors. After passing the ticket

Left Metro entrances in the city centre soon became known as 'Fosteritos' after the architect Norman Foster. Instead of the traditional <M> used in Madrid or Barcelona, the Bilbao metro chose three red rings symbolising the tunnel and the wheels of the train. This is the entrance to Moyua Station.

Below Exits were designed as straight to the surface as possible to avoid loss of orientation. Although there are no escalators between vestibule and platforms, these take you directly to street level at Moyua.

barrier zone, he can overlook the whole platform area. There are no hidden areas. Materials are limited to concrete, glass and stainless steel, all three used in their natural state. Together with Norman Foster, Otl Aicher created the *Metro Bilbao* corporate image, designing a new letter type called Rotis Semisans (named after a small village in southern Germany where Aicher retired), used in all written expressions like signposting, station name panels, or publications like *metroberri*. Where possible internationally understood pictograms were used, in order to avoid excessive bilinguism (Spanish and Basque). The only colours used are red, black and white, and different shades of grey. Unlike the elsewhere popular <M> (traditionally in a diamond) to mark station accesses on the surface, three red circles on a high mast were chosen as the Bilbao metro logo.

The first extension of the initial line from Casco Viejo to Bolueta (1.8km with three stations) was put into service on 5 July 1997. It serves the populated areas of Santutxu, and provides a comfortable transfer to the *EuskoTren* suburban lines to Bermeo and Gernika regional trains to Donostia / San Sebastián. One year later a new elevator was built at Santutxu station which quickly carries up to 24 people from the 40m deep station to the surface.

A few months before the opening of the Casco Viejo – Bolueta section, construction on the first 6km section of Line 2 started between San Inazio and Urbinaga, for opening in October 2001.

CONSTRUCTION OF THE METRO

In order to create an attractive metro line, stations had to be built as close as possible to the surface. To save energy, stations should lie higher than the running tunnel in between, so that trains automatically lose speed when entering the station and accelerate faster when leaving. To avoid problems with foundations of buildings along the route, the line runs beneath broad avenues where possible.

The Bilbao Metro was constructed mainly by NATM (new Austrian tunnelling method), although for some stretches (2.3km) the cut-and-cover method was applied, and for one river crossing prefabricated elements were used. Bilbao's soil is formed by rocks of a quite uniform composition, which are easy to excavate by machines. These marlstones consist of clay and quartz particles with calcium carbonate cements, crystals and pyrite nodules, with only few fossil remains. Along the river Nervión, which winds through the city, less compact quaternary deposits, loam, gravel, sand and lime are found.

Using NATM for excavating both running tunnels and stations in the city centre of Bilbao, largely helped to reduce the impact on everyday life on the surface. The only problem was where to establish a work base to access the tunnels. One was dug at Plaza Moyua in the heart of the Ensanche and the other one near San Nicolás in the old part of the city. Considered unsuitable for soft soil, NATM seemed ideal for Bilbao's rock soils. This method based on a constant dialogue with the terrain does not necessarily need covering of tunnel walls, although in most cases sprayed concrete, steel meshes or metal ribs are used to protect the tunnel from water infiltration, and to stabilise the rock formations around it. The actual digging is done by roadheaders. All stations (100m long, 18m wide by 13m high) from BASARRATE to DEUSTO and from GURUTZETA to BAGATZA were excavated this way.

Apart from some short stretches, the cut-and-cover method was applied mainly along Lehendakari Aguirre Avenue and Iruña street in Deusto, where rocks are deeper than the metro tunnel, and for station and tunnel entrances (near BOLUETA and SAN INAZIO). SARRIKO, SAN INAZIO, ERANDIO, AREETA and ALGORTA underground stations were built by the cut-and-cover method. The most interesting of these is SARRIKO for its immense size with a huge glass entrance on the surface that lets daylight come into the station.

The two crossings under the River Nervión along the original line were the most spectacular parts of the construction process. To build these sections, NATM was discarded, because this would have placed the nearby stations too deep. Therefore for the section between SAN MAMÉS and DEUSTO, the technique of immersed tunnels was chosen, a technique used for the first time in Spain. Two 86m prefabricated concrete caissons (made in a provisional dry dock in Deusto) were floated to their final position and then lowered into a trench in the river bed.

The other river crossing between ABANDO and CASCO VIEJO had to be carried out in a different way, because the river is too narrow in this section and there was no space to build a dry dock. The

CASCO VIEJO – the entrance from Unamuno square in the heart of the old city leads only slightly downwards, but deep into the mountain.

river bed partly consists of rock, but also permeable gravel which had to be turned into a compact material by means of jet-grouting before excavation could be started. This way a resistant vault was formed, under which the tunnel could be bored. After that the NATM was applied and the excavated tunnel was totally lined with concrete.

NATM was also chosen for the construction of Line 2 which began in spring 1997, even for the 45m deep crossing under the River Nervión, as the distance between the two stations, San Inazio and Gurutzeta / Cruces, allowed a deeper alignment through solid rock. This third river crossing was finished in September 1999. The area around Ansio was built by *cut-and-cover,* thus creating an easy access to the construction site. Some of the material excavated along this route was used for the harbour expansion at Santurtzi carried out at the same time. Station design along the new line follows the standards established for Line 1, in order to continue the uniform look of the entire metro network which has become a landmark for the city and its surrounding county.

BILBAO METRO – OPERATION & FARE SYSTEM

On weekdays the Bilbao Metro operates from 06:00 to 23:00 at these basic frequencies:

Bolueta – San Inazio	... ...	every 5 minutes
further to Bidezabal	... ...	every 10 minutes (5 minutes rush hours)
further to Larrabasterra	...	every 20 minutes (10 minutes rush hours)
and through to Plentzia	...	every 20 minutes
San Inazio – Urbinaga	... ...	every 5–10 minutes

On Fridays and the day before public holidays service is extended until 02:00 every 30 minutes between Bolueta and Plentzia. On Saturdays there is a special night service: every 30 minutes from 23:00–06:00 (the only metro service in Spain operating all night on Saturdays). On Sundays and public holidays there is a train every 10 minutes between Bolueta and San Inazio / Urbinaga, and every 20 minutes between San Inazio and Plentzia.

During the summer months, *Metro Bilbao* operates a bus service from Plentzia station to Gorliz and Armintza with buses every 20 minutes which can be used with a Zone C metro ticket. During that season metro service is also increased to a 5–10 minutes interval as far as Sopelana.

The Bilbao metro is divided into three fare zones:

Zone A:	Bolueta – Astrabudua / Urbinaga
Zone B:	Leioa – Berango
Zone C:	Larrabasterra – Plentzia

San Mamés – a typical vestibule – tickets have to be bought from vending machines and have to be introduced into the validating machines when entering and when leaving the metro due to a 3-zone fare system.

Tickets

(Prices shown in € Euro valid for 2000 and only valid on the Metro):

Ocasional (Single):

1 zone	€0.84
2 zones	€0.99
3 zones	€1.17

Bonometro (10 trips):

1 zone	€5.16
2 zones	€6.13
3 zones	€7.36

Bono Plus (10 trips for people over 65 or the handicapped):

any number of zones	€2.04

Mensual (Monthly Pass):

1 zone	€21.63
2 zones	€26.14
3 zones	€31.25

Super 50 (50 trips within 30 days):

1 zone	€17.80
2 zones	€21.18
3 zones	€25.39

Billete Joven (Yearly Pass for young people up to 26 years):

1 zone	€138.23
2 zones	€165.27
3 zones	€198.33

Metro Dinero (Cash card): ... €24.00

For the ever growing number of tourists a new day-pass was introduced in February 2000:

Billete 1 día
(valid for unlimited travel within one day in all 3 zones): ... €3.00.

With 44 per cent Bonometro is the most popular ticket while the monthly pass is only used by 14 per cent of all passengers.

Since 1998 transfer tickets between metro and *EuskoTren* suburban services have been on offer. Prices are according to the distance travelled. The choice is between a 10-rides ticket, a monthly pass or a yearly pass for the young. These tickets can be bought at *EuskoTren* stations. In 1999 similar transfer tickets were introduced for the *Renfe Cercanías* services within the municipality of Bilbao. A combined ticket is also available for metro and bus shuttle from Leioa station to the University campus.

Tickets can only be bought from ticket vending machines. The magnetic cards must be cancelled when entering the pay zone. A valid ticket automatically opens the access doors (similar to those seen on the Paris Metro). When leaving the metro area tickets have to be introduced into the slot again to check whether the correct fare zone has been paid. With this double control, fraud is very low on the Bilbao Metro. Travelling without a ticket is fined with €30.

Along Line 1 there are three Customers' Offices, at Casco Viejo, San Inazio and Areeta. Here general information and season tickets can be obtained, and personal ID cards necessary for season tickets are issued. They also sell souvenir items.

Although very popular from the very beginning, Bilbao's metro has had rising passenger numbers since its opening in November 1995:

1996	31.6million passengers
1997	41.5million (with 3 new stations from July 1997)
1998	49.1million
1999	50.8million.

With more than 4million passengers a year, ABANDO, CASCO VIEJO, MOYUA, INDAUTXU and DEUSTO are the top five stations along Line 1, followed by AREETA, SANTUTXU and SAN MAMÉS. Among the least frequented are LUTXANA, LAMIAKO, BERANGO and URDULIZ with less than 300,000 each. On 15 May 1998 the metro reached a record when it transported 234,000 on a single day, the day Athletic de Bilbao qualified for the Soccer Champions League. This record was beaten on 21 December 1999 (Santo Tomás, a traditional Basque market) with 245,000 passengers.

It is also interesting to observe that more than 60 per cent of all trips are done within price Zone A (basically the city of Bilbao) which means that, although the line has a very suburban character especially in Zone C, the metro is fully justifiable as an intra-urban means of transport.

In order to permanently improve service, *METRO BILBAO* established the so-called *Panel Metro Bilbao* which consists of more than 700 regular passengers, who return a continuous feedback on the service provided by the metro operator.

About four times a year, *METRO BILBAO* publishes a free newspaper called *metroberri* which is distributed among passengers and includes the latest news concerning the metro and its future. For the young ones, the mascot *Lurpi* (which means 'underground' in Basque) was created.

BILBAO METRO – ROLLING STOCK

On 11 November 1995, 16 trains (UT 501–516) started operating on Line 1. This number was increased to 24 trains (UT 517–524) which were delivered gradually by CAF/ABB during the first half of 1996. In early 1999, Metro Bilbao ordered 10 new trains from CAF/Adtranz to be delivered for service on Line 2 from October 2001. Three more trains were added to the order in spring 2000.

One metro unit consists of four motor cars, all of which are connected with full-width gangways allowing passengers to move freely between cars. The carriages at both ends include a driver's cabin and are 17.8m long, while the intermediate open-end carriages are 17.3m long – thus a 4-car unit has a total length of 72m. All carriages rest on two bogies. Although 1000mm gauge is used, trains are 2.80m wide. There are three doors per car at either side of the train. One train can accomodate 144 seated passengers and up to 568 standing (six people per square metre). All trains are air-conditioned. If necessary in the future, a trailer can be added in the middle of the train. The 1500Vdc electric train units use overhead power collection. Like the Madrid Metro, the Bilbao Metro is operated on the left, at a maximum speed of 80km/h.

When Line 1 opened in 1995 there were several level crossings along the surface line taken over from *Eusko Trenbideak*. These were all gradually eliminated, and by 1998 the whole line was fenced off in order to install ATP (automatic train protection) and ATO (automatic train operation), the common standard for metro train operation around the world, in which the driver only presses a button to close the doors and to set the train in motion. Acceleration and braking is controlled by a centralised computer.

The 1000mm gauge does not mean smaller trains. Metro carriages are 2.8m wide and offer a spacious and comfortable interior. Passengers can walk freely from one end of the train to the other.

OTHER RAIL TRANSPORT IN THE BILBAO METROPOLITAN AREA

Renfe Cercanías/Aldirikoak

Three suburban lines are operated by *Renfe* (Spanish National Railways) from the centre of Bilbao. Until 4 March 1999 the Muskiz and Santurtzi lines (C–1 and C–2) terminated at La Naja which was quite close to Abando, Bilbao's Central Railway Station, but no through service was possible. Therefore a former link line (the so-called *Variante Sur*) between Olabeaga and Abando was rebuilt to connect the two northern lines (Muskiz and Santurtzi lines) to the southern line to Orduña (C–3), thus creating a new multifunctional transfer station at San Mamés (*Metro* and *TermiBus*), a joint station with *FEVE* at Ametzola and two new intermediate stations at Autonomía and Zabalburu. Around Autonomía and Ametzola the old line was covered to create a new avenue. As Abando is a terminal station, passengers have to change trains here to continue. Within Bilbao, a new station will be built at La Peña on the southern line C–3, between Abando and Ollargan.

Once this new line was in operation, the former route along the river between the Guggenheim Museum and La Naja next to Arenal bridge was dismantled, although on the remaining section between Olabeaga and Parke-Guggenheim a shuttle service is maintained as long as the new development area of Abandoibarra between the Guggenheim Museum and the new Euskalduna Congress and Concert Hall allows this option.

From 2002 a tram line from San Mamés via Abandoibarra along the river to the city centre at Arriaga Theatre and further on to Atxuri (*EuskoTren* Station) will provide service along this corridor. In December 1999, *Renfe* proposed a new service along this section, with a short tunnel from San Mamés station to Euskalduna, and then along the still existing tracks to the Guggenheim Museum.

The *Renfe Cercanías* service operates an irregular timetable, and is quite busy on the line to Santurtzi (C–1: trains every 6–10 minutes during rush hours, 30–60 minutes on Sundays), to Muskiz (C–2: every 20–30 minutes) and less so on the Orduña line (C–3: 30–60 minutes interval).

A *Renfe Cercanías* train was still running past the Guggenheim Museum in summer 1998 on a service from La Naja to Santurtzi. This corridor will be served by a modern tram line from 2001 onwards.

This *EuskoTren* unit has just arrived at San Ignacio from Lezama. From here the original line used to continue to Plentzia. Now there is no direct transfer to the metro here, San Inazio metro station lies some 500m to the west.

EuskoTren

The Basque Railways operate two lines in the Bilbao area. One uses the remaining stretch of the former Plentzia line between San Ignacio and Casco Viejo / Zazpi Kaleak (double track and partly in tunnels). At Casco Viejo a new station complex was built to allow transfer to the metro. From here trains run through to Lezama on single track. Service is every 30 minutes with some extra trains during rush hours in lecture periods, as this line gives direct access to the University of Deusto.

At San Ignacio transfer to the metro is not possible. Although both stations carry the same name they lie some 500m from each other.

The second line starts at Atxuri and runs via a new transfer station with Metro Bilbao at Bolueta out to Lemoa (15 minutes interval) where the line splits into a branch to Gernika / Bermeo and another one to Durango / Ermua (both branches served every 30 minutes). On the latter branch there is also a through-service to Eibar and Donostia / San Sebastián.

FEVE

FEVE (*Ferrocarriles de Vía Estrecha* – Narrow Gauge Railways) operates and reopens some narrow gauge lines along the Spanish northern coast (for example Bilbao – Santander – Oviedo). One branch is operated as a suburban service from Bilbao to Balmaseda with a 30–60 minute headway with four stations within the built-up metropolitan area of Bilbao (Bilbao-Concordia station which

FEVE train at its Bilbao terminus Concordia near Abando.

is situated close to ABANDO and actually on top of the former La Naja station, AMETZOLA, BASURTO and ZORROTZA). In the near future, a 1km long section and BASURTO station will be put underground and a new station will be built at Elejabarri.

Funicular de Artxanda

From Plaza del Funicular, near the new pedestrian bridge Zubizuri (White Bridge), and for less than €1 this funicular takes you up the mountain of Artxanda from where one has a tremendous view over Bilbao and its surroundings.

Puente de Vizcaya – Bizkaia Zubia: The Hanging Bridge

Another very special means of transport in the Greater Bilbao area is the Hanging Bridge between Portugalete and Areeta (Las Arenas). This kind of ferry suspended from a huge iron structure is over 100 years old and transports people and cars across the river Nervión every few minutes for only E0.30. Apart from so called *gasolinas* (ferry boats) this was the only connection between the two river banks outside Bilbao until 1985 when a motorway bridge was built.

Right The Biskaia Hanging Bridge links both sides of the Ría de Bilbao (Portugalete – Areeta). For many years this suspended ferry was the only river crossing outside Bilbao.

PROJECTS FOR THE FUTURE

Public transportation is quite good in Bilbao, but integration of different systems – metro, suburban trains and buses – has only just begun. Some tickets are available which allow passengers to use both metro and *EUSKOTREN* services, or metro and *RENFE CERCANÍAS* (only within Bilbao city). In 2000 a new system called *Creditrans* was introduced which will ultimately be valid for all transit operators and include passes for unlimited travel on all trains and buses. New transfer stations have been built at BOLUETA, CASCO VIEJO, ABANDO, AMETZOLA or SAN MAMÉS showing that the process is going in the right direction. The information system has still to be unified, with maps showing all operators.

After the positive experience observed in Valencia and many other European cities, Bilbao seems to incline itself towards the construction of light metro (metro ligero) or modern tramway lines, partly by transforming existing rail corridors or by building new lines.

The conversion of the *RENFE* suburban line to SANTURTZI (C–1) into a light rail line when metro Line 2 has reached there is being discussed, although conversion cannot start until around 2010.

Apart from the above mentioned tramway line from SAN MAMÉS to ATXURI along the river (scheduled to open in 2002), the *EUSKOTREN* line from SAN IGNACIO to LEZAMA could also be converted into a light rail line in the long term, with new branches to Leioa (University campus), Lutxana (along the existing disused rail link), the airport and the Technology Park.

A light rail line will also serve the districts of Otxarkoaga and Rekaldeberri, originally planned to be linked by a third metro line.

BIBLIOGRAPHY AND RELATED WEBSITES

Madrid

Azorín García. Francisco. **Madrid y el metro caminan juntos.** Madrid: Rubiños, 1997 *in Spanish.* ISBN 84-8041-096-5.

Moya, Aurora. **Metro de Madrid 1919–1989: setenta años de historia.** Madrid: Metro de Madrid, 1990 *in Spanish.* ISBN 84-404-8285-X.

Barcelona

Cabana, F. **Estacions.** Barcelona: Lunwerg, 1998 *in Catalan.* ISBN 84-7782-522-X.

Catalunya. Dirección General de Transports. **Metro de Barcelona: manual de senyalització.** Barcelona: Generalitat de Catalunya, 1984 *in Catalan.* ISBN 84-393-0501-X.

Salmerón i Bosch, Carles. **El Metro de Barcelona: història del ferrocarril metropolità de Barcelona.**, Barcelona: C. Salmerón, 1992. (Els trens de Catalunya 16) *in Catalan.* ISBN 84-604-2387-5.

Salmerón i Bosch, Carles. **El Metro de Barcelona – II: història i tècnica.** Barcelona: C. Salmerón, 1992. (Els Trens de Catalunya 17) *in Catalan.* ISBN 84-604-4886-X.

Salmerón i Bosch, Carles. **El Tren de Sarrià: història del ferrocarril Barcelona – Sarrià.** Barcelona: C. Salmerón, 1988. (Els trens de Catalunya 13a) *in Catalan.* ISBN 84-404-3105-8.

Salmerón i Bosch, Carles. **Els Ferrocarrils Catalans-I-III.** Barcelona: C. Salmerón, 1989. (Els trens de Catalunya 5 6A, 6B) *in Catalan.* ISBN 84-404-5716-2

Salmerón i Bosch, Carles. **Els Ferrocarrils de Catalunya.** Barcelona: C. Salmerón, 1989, (Els trens de Catalunya 13B) *in Catalan.*

Alemany i Llovera, Joan; Mestre, Jesús. **Els transports a l'àrea de Barcelona: diligències, tramvies, autobusos i metro.** Barcelona: TMB, 1986 *in Catalan.* ISBN 84-85905-3-0.

Espinàs, Josep M. **Els noms de les estacions del metro.** – Barcelona: TMB, 1988 *in Catalan or Spanish.* ISBN 84-404-2754-9.

Ubach i Soler, Tomàs M. **El ferrocarril: La xarxa catalana.** Barcelona: Ketres, 1984 *in Catalan.* ISBN 84-85256-39-5.

Valencia

Alcaide González, Rafael. **El trenet de Valencia.** Barcelona: Edición Lluís Prieto, 1998. (Monografías del Ferrocarril 9) *in Spanish.* ISBN 84-921005-8-3.

Bilbao

Barañano Letamendia, Kosme María de; Presmanes Arizmendi, Agustín; Medinaveitia Foronda, José Ramón. **Metro Bilbao: ingeniería y arquitectura = Ingeniaritzako eta arkitekturak.** – Vitoria-Gasteiz: Imebisa, 1998 *in Spanish and Basque, and in Spanish and English.* ISBN 84-923479-0-2.

Barañano, Kosme María de; González de Durana, Javier. **Metro de Bilbao: proyectos de arquitectura.** Vitoria: Departamento de Transportes y Obras Públicas del Gobierno Vasco, 1989 *in Spanish.* ISBN 84-71542-684-0.

Sevilla

Justo Alpañés, José Luis de. **Pasado y futuro del metro de Sevilla.** Sevilla: Universidad de Sevilla, 1994 *in Spanish.* ISBN 84-472-0179-1.

RAILWAY MAGAZINES

Vía Libre (monthly magazine published by Fundación de los Ferrocarriles Españoles)
Carril (published by Associación d'Amics del Ferrocarril de Barcelona)

WEBSITES

most of them offer an English version

metroPlanet
- A Guide to all the World's Underground Networks – in English by Robert Schwandl
www.metropla.net

Metro de Madrid
www.metromadrid.es

Consorcio de Transportes de Madrid
www.ctm-madrid.es

ATM – Autoritat del Transport Metropolità (Barcelona)
www.atm-transmet.es

Metro de Barcelona
www.tmb.net

Ferrocarrils de la Generalitat de Catalunya (Catalan Railways)
www.fgc.catalunya.net

Ferrocarrils de la Generalitat Valenciana (Valencia Railways)
www.cop.gva.es/fgv/

Metro Bilbao
www.metrobilbao.net

EuskoTren (Basque Railways)
www.jet.es/euskotren/

Renfe Cercanías (Suburban Railways)
www.renfe.es/empresa/cercanias/

Fundación de los Ferrocarriles Españoles (Spanish Railway Association)
www.ffe.es

CD-ROM

– Schwandl, Robert. **Metros in Spain on CD = Metros de España en CD.** Barcelona: metroplanet, 2000. Includes more pictures, maps, sounds, etc.
Details at http://www.metropla.net/spain/cdrom.htm

ONLINE-NEWSPAPERS

which provide an easy search for metro news

w3.el-mundo.es (Madrid)
www2.vanguardia.es (Barcelona)
www.avui.com (Barcelona)
www.levante-emv.com (Valencia)
www.lasprovincias.es (Valencia)
www.elcorreodigital.com (Bilbao)
www.diariovasco.com (Bilbao)

SUMMARY OF SPANISH METROS

Madrid

Line	Length (km)	Stations	Single tickets	Monthly Travelcard (Central Zone)
L–1	16.7	27		
L–2	7.9	15		
+R	+1.1	+2		
L–3	6.4	11		
L–4	12.8	20		
L–5	18.2	27		
L–6	23.5	27		
L–7	18.8	22		
L–8	8.0	4		
L–9	20.0 +18.0[1]	22 +4[1]		
L–10	17.7	17		
L–11	2.3	3		
Total	**171.4**	**201**	**€0.81**	**€27.83**

Barcelona

Line	Length (km)	Stations	Single tickets	Monthly Travelcard
L1	20.7	30		
L2	8.6	12		
L3 [2]	16.6	24		
L4	21.2	26		
L5	16.6	22		
U6+U7	7.0	13		
Total	**88.3**	**124**	**€0.90**	**€33.43**

Valencia

Line	Length (km)	Stations	Single tickets	Monthly Travelcard
L–1 urban	8.3	11		
L–3 urban	9.7	12		
Total	**18.0**	**23**	**€0.78**	**€27.10**

Bilbao

Line	Length (km)	Stations	Single tickets	Monthly Travelcard
L–1	22.3	27		
L–2 [2]	5.9	5		
Total	**28.2**	**32**	**€0.84**	**€21.63** (metro only)

[1] suburban section
[2] includes sections opening in 2001